In the Footsteps
of Stonewall Jackson

D0088554

973.7 J63i
Johnson, Clint.
In the footsteps of
  Stonewall Jackson   12.95

Also by Clint Johnson

In the Footsteps of Robert E. Lee
Touring Virginia's and West Virginia's Civil War Sites
Touring the Carolinas' Civil War Sites
Civil War Blunders

In the Footsteps
of Stonewall Jackson

by
Clint Johnson

John F. Blair, Publisher   *Winston-Salem, North Carolina*

Published by John F. Blair, Publisher

*The paper in this book meets the guidelines
for permanence and durability of the
Committee on Production Guidelines for
Book Longevity of the Council on Library Resources.*

Cover Photographs:
Painting of Stonewall Jackson courtesy of The Library of Congress
Bottom row left to right: The original grave site of Jackson,
the V. M. I. barracks, the Boyd House in Bunker Hill

Library of Congress Cataloging-in-Publication Data

Johnson, Clint, 1953–
In the footsteps of Stonewall Jackson / by Clint Johnson.
      p.   cm.
Includes bibliographical references and index.
ISBN 0-89587-244-7 (alk. paper)
1. Jackson, Stonewall, 1824 –1863—Homes and haunts—Guidebooks.
2. Historic sites—West Virginia—Guidebooks. 3. Historic sites—
Virginia—Guidebooks. 4. Historic sites—Maryland—Guidebooks. 5.
Jackson, Stonewall, 1824–1863—Anecdotes. 6. Generals—Confederate
States of America—Biography—Anecdotes. 7. West Virginia—
Guidebooks. 8. Virginia—Guidebooks. 9.Maryland—Guidebooks. 10.
North America—Guidebooks. I. Title.
E467.1.J15 J64 2002
917.5404'44—dc21
2001049951

Design by Debra Long Hampton

Dedication

This book is dedicated to two of my ancestors who probably wished they had served under Stonewall Jackson.

One was Lieutenant Augustus Milledge Hartsfield of the Fourth Georgia Sharpshooters, who survived Chickamauga, Georgia, only to be captured at Missionary Ridge, Tennessee, several weeks later. He spent two years in a Union prison camp called Johnson's Island. He died young after the war following a short career as a surveyor.

The other was Captain Richard Newton Moore of Hilliard's Legion of Alabama. He was mortally wounded charging up Snodgrass Hill at Chickamauga at the head of his company. His regiment suffered 72 percent killed and wounded. He left several young children, one of whom was my great-grandmother.

Why do these two ancestors of mine wish from their graves that they had served under Stonewall Jackson? Because both of them served under General Braxton Bragg. If you read Civil War history, that is answer enough.

Map Index

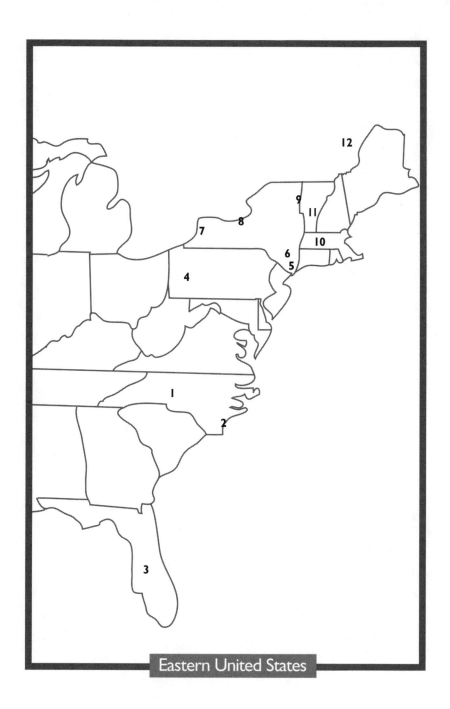

Eastern United States

Contents

Preface

When I finished *In the Footsteps of Robert E. Lee* in 2000, I felt I had a fairly good handle on what motivated the commanding general of the Army of Northern Virginia: devotion to God, to family, to principles, and to his home state of Virginia. I believed I knew Lee after reading and researching his life.

I cannot say the same thing about Thomas J. "Stonewall" Jackson.

Even after reading several biographies and books about the battles in which he participated, then visiting the sites important in his life, I still can't say that I've figured him out. I doubt anyone can truly say they understand Jackson.

The man was a brilliant general, perhaps the best tactician on either side. He did more with less than any other general. He got his men to perform miracles of physical performance that have not been duplicated before or since in military history. No general, with the exception of Robert E. Lee, was more loved than "Old Jack" (the name he preferred, if he had to go by a nickname).

Yet for all the battlefield victories, some things about Jackson just do not add up.

How did he win so many battles when he was such a poor judge of military talent? In case after case, Jackson seems to have picked staff members—and sometimes generals—based on their religiousness, rather than on the administrative talents they brought to the table. Many of his most trusted staff members had no management experience at all, never having served in the military or even in a business. Jackson once gave his chief of staff (who had been his chaplain) vague orders to load his army on trains and move it secretly toward Richmond. Jackson never told his professional generals where the army was going, but he told this former chaplain.

Why did Jackson favor some poor-performing officers over better-performing men? He once promoted a major to general because he had known the man in Lexington, not because he had shown any leadership skills on the battlefield. He once promoted a Marylander to take charge of Jackson's old Stonewall Brigade. That man was hated so much by common soldiers in the brigade that they threatened to murder him on the battlefield.

Why did Jackson pay such attention to petty matters? He often would arrest or threaten to arrest officers who defied him. He once arrested one of his best generals for marching his men longer than 50 minutes in an hour. Jackson once demanded to know why an officer had not met him at a specific time. Even though the officer explained he had gotten lost, Jackson ignored the explanation and asked again: Why was the general late when he had been ordered to be on time?

Why did Jackson keep his military goals to himself to the point of ridiculousness? For example, he rarely told his division commanders—his seconds-in-command—where the march that day was going, much less what they were expected to do once they got to their destination. Jackson would station couriers at crossroads to point generals in the direction they were supposed to march their men. Once, Jackson ordered his quartermaster to point the head of the wagon train toward the Valley Turnpike. The quartermaster subsequently asked a simple, reasonable question of his leader: Since they would be leaving the next morning, in which direction should he point the head of the wagon train, north or south? Jackson's answer was that the quartermaster had been ordered to point the wagons in the direction of the turnpike, and that he should do as he was told.

No one can accurately psychoanalyze a man who has been dead nearly 140 years to explain why he acted the way he did. All we can do is look at Jackson's record and marvel at how successful he was. Even considering his failures—including spectacular ones such as the Seven Days' Campaign—there is no argument that he was one of the greatest generals in history. No one, not even Robert E. Lee, had a military track record like Jackson's. Though Jackson lost some battles, just hearing the name *Stonewall* could start dozens of Union generals and thousands of Union soldiers quaking in their boots.

All I can do is point readers in the right direction to find sites associated with the general. I cannot and will not attempt to explain why Jackson was such a fantastic commander. I'll leave that to the professional historians and to your own reasoning.

This book looks only at Jackson sites in the United States and Canada. I have not tried to find the sites associated with him in Mexico, due to the difficulty of travel and the difference in language. Neither have I tried to track his European vacation. Jackson spent weeks on the European continent but left bare details in his letters home about what he visited. The book begins with the "core" states of West Virginia, Virginia, and Maryland, where Jackson spent most of his life or fought his major military battles. It then moves south to sites in North Carolina and Florida, then north to sites stretching from Pennsylvania to Canada.

Some sites are on private property, so please do not trespass. Let my descriptions and photographs satisfy your interest.

The image of Jackson has remained almost mythical in the minds of most people who read about him, despite the best efforts of the historical revisionists working overtime to bring down Confederate heroes.

Will anyone ever figure out Stonewall Jackson? No.

Will anyone ever succeed in destroying the image of Stonewall Jackson as a Southern hero? Maybe. The politically motivated forces wanting to obliterate the South as a distinct region and to wipe out the memory of the Confederacy are powerful and well funded. The only people aligned against those interests are average citizens who seek balance and historical accuracy. That means you, dear reader, "are in for it," to quote Jackson when he saw the enemy arrayed against him at Kernstown, Virginia.

It is an uneven fight, to be sure, but just the sort of battle in which Jackson and his men thrived and prevailed.

Acknowledgments

As with every Civil War travel book I have written, I must start by thanking local historians. Without these people, there would not be any history left in a country that sometimes seems bent on destroying everything with a past in order to live in the moment.

Thanks to Anna Bainbridge of Ivy, Virginia, for helping me find the location of Mechum's River Station, a now-abandoned railway station where Jackson's men boarded the train in order to move quickly to what would become the McDowell battlefield, and from which Jackson left the Shenandoah Valley on his way to the Seven Days' Battles east of Richmond.

Thanks to Paul Beatty of Duke Energy for showing me around the site of Cottage Home, the Morrison family homeplace in Lincoln County, North Carolina. It is now located at the entrance to a Duke Energy electric power plant.

Thanks to Jan Blodgett, archivist at Davidson College in North Carolina, for finding a historian who knew details about D. H. Hill's life at Davidson.

Thanks to Bill Boyd, a "pard" in my reenactment group, the 26th North Carolina Troops Reactivated, for traveling with me to read maps and keep me company. Bill is the sort of guy to have along when you have to knock on strangers' doors to ask for information. He looks harmless and can charm his way into a home.

Thanks to the Reverend Tina Cox of Gordonsville Presbyterian Church in Virginia for showing me the pew where Jackson slept during services. Not to worry, Reverend Cox. He slept through every church service he ever attended, not just those in Gordonsville.

Thanks to Tom Darro, vice president of communications for the Niagara Falls Convention and Visitors Bureau, for his help in finding what currently occupies the former site of the old Cataract Hotel, where Jackson spent two honeymoons.

Thanks to Dr. Chris Fonvielle of Wilmington, North Carolina, an accomplished author on the Civil War, for finding the obituary of Colonel John Barry, the man who ordered the volley that wounded Jackson.

Thanks to Colonel Keith Gibson of the V.M.I. Museum in Lexington, Virginia, for providing details on the cannon battery in front of Jackson's statue and on some of the artifacts in the museum.

Thanks to Francisco Jardin, director of the Harbor Defense Museum at Fort Hamilton in Brooklyn, New York, for gathering old maps and accounts of the fort to see if any quarters used by Jackson still stand. All of the quarters were located under what is now the Verrazano Narrows Bridge approach.

Thanks to Rodney K. Kunath of Northampton, Massachusetts, for information on water cures, especially the Round Hill Water Cure, which Jackson proclaimed the best he ever tried.

Thanks to Dr. Malcom Lester, professor emeritus at Davidson College, for help in tracking sites around Davidson associated with D. H. Hill, Jackson's brother-in-law. Unfortunately, the house where a nervous Jackson spent his last days before marriage no longer stands.

Thanks to Royster Lyle, a descendant of the man who ran a bookstore in Lexington that became a favorite haunt of Professor Jackson's. With Royster's help, I figured out what building likely was the home of Lyle's Book Store, a place that helped make Jackson a more rounded person.

Thanks to Lisa McCown, special collections assistant at the Washington and Lee University Library in Lexington, for helping look for the address of the house where D. H. Hill and his wife were living when Professor Thomas J. Jackson first laid eyes on Anna Morrison, his future second wife. I never managed to uncover the address of this romantic house, proving there is still a little mystery about the life of Stonewall Jackson.

Thanks to Tiffany Miller and Robbie Robertson, managers of the Young Life Camp at Rockbridge Alum Springs, Virginia, for giving me a tour of one of the few resorts still in existence that was visited by both Robert E. Lee and Stonewall Jackson.

Thanks to Jeanne Mozier of Bath, West Virginia, for help in determining where Stonewall and his brigade camped when they invaded Bath in 1861.

Thanks to Megan Haley Newman, curator at the Stonewall Jackson House in Lexington, for her help in finding sites associated with Jackson in the city where he finally found happiness.

Thanks to Bev Packard of the Brattleboro Chamber of Commerce for details on the water-cure establishment in the little Vermont town that Jackson visited.

Thanks to Nancy Phillips of the Loudoun County Convention and Visitors Bureau for describing the locations of Big Spring and the Henry Harrison House in Leesburg, Virginia.

Thanks to Robert Pirani, director of environmental programs at the Regional Plan Association in New York City, for his help in learning more about future plans for Governors Island.

Thanks to Color Sergeant Randy Price of the 26th North Carolina Troops Reactivated, my boss on the reenacting battlefield, as I am senior color corporal. Randy helped find Cottage Home, the place in North Carolina where Professor Thomas J. Jackson married Anna Morrison.

Thanks to Sandy Soderberg of the Clarke School for the Deaf in Northampton, Massachusetts, for her help in securing information about the area when it was home to the Round Hill Water Cure and for putting me together with Rodney Kunath.

Thanks to Joy Gilchrist Stalnaker of Weston, West Virginia, for her help in tracking down sites around Jackson's boyhood home, including the grave of Gibson Butcher, the young man who left West Point and opened a slot for Jackson.

Thanks to Bob Williams, one of my reenacting "pards" in the 26th North Carolina Regiment Reactivated, for showing me the route Jackson took to begin his portion of the Seven Days' Battles. Bob and I have reenacted together since 1978, when we were both Floridians.

Thanks to Alice Williams, executive director of the Rockbridge County Historical Society, for showing me the collection of Stonewall Jackson items and helping figure out where Lyle's Book Store was in downtown Lexington.

Thanks to Siri Wright and Lynn Compton of the Exchange Hotel Museum in Gordonsville, Virginia, for trying to help figure out where the Garnett court-martial was held at Liberty Mills outside Orange.

Thanks to the staff of the Orange County Historical Society for attempting to find the house used by General Dick Ewell as a head-quarters at Liberty Mills. We never found it mentioned in any source, again proving that there is still some mystery about the life of Stone-wall Jackson.

Thanks again to the staff of John F. Blair, Publisher, in Winston-Salem, North Carolina, for continuing to back me in these book ventures. Just when writer and publisher think we have finally tapped out the Civil War history market, we figure out something else that has not been covered. This is the fifth book I have written for them, and I hope to follow it with many more in the future.

Thanks to my wife, Barbara, who complains that she sometimes takes pictures for my books and never gets photo credit. Here it is: Thanks to Barbara for all the pictures she took for my previous books. (I don't believe she took a single photo for this one.) Barbara has stood by me patiently since 1984, most significantly when I tore all of the ligaments in my knee just before we were both going out to look for jobs in 1987. I especially appreciate her understanding during all those times when I came home with some new Civil War book or piece of reenacting equipment. She was teased repeatedly about being the first Yankee (Wisconsin-born, so close enough) in my family in 230 years, until I discovered my cousins also had spouses of the Northern persuasion. Through it all, she has stayed with me. We've remained close since our marriage in 1984. That will never change.

And finally, thanks again to Frances Pooser, my fourth-grade teacher in Arcadia, Florida, for telling a thrilling story about the Battle of Natural Bridge, Florida, a tiny fight between regular United States soldiers and a militia made up of old men and young boys. The militia won. She touched a nerve that led to an interest that has consumed me for 40 years.

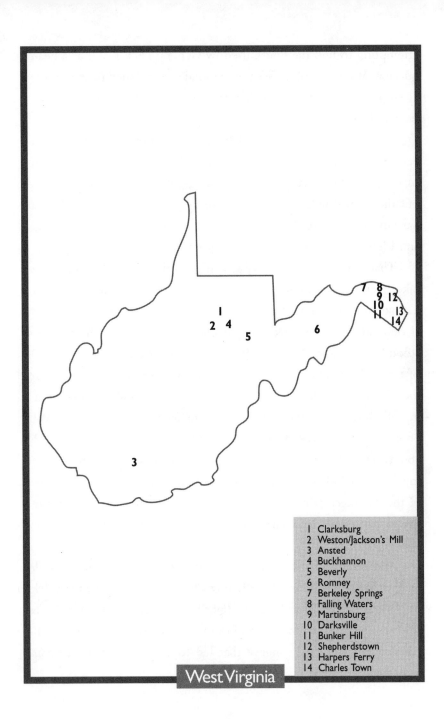

1 Clarksburg
2 Weston/Jackson's Mill
3 Ansted
4 Buckhannon
5 Beverly
6 Romney
7 Berkeley Springs
8 Falling Waters
9 Martinsburg
10 Darksville
11 Bunker Hill
12 Shepherdstown
13 Harpers Ferry
14 Charles Town

West Virginia

Clarksburg

Clarksburg is located at the intersection of I-79 and US 50 in northern West Virginia.

It is somehow fitting that the birthplace of the orphan who would grow up to be one of America's most unusual military figures no longer exists. If not for a very particular set of circumstances, it seems unlikely that anyone outside Clarksburg, Virginia (now West Virginia), would have ever cared about the life of Thomas Jackson. Certainly, no one would have bothered to erect a brass plaque on a downtown office building over the spot where his birthplace once stood.

The plaque is on the wall of a building on the north side of Main Street a half-block west of the courthouse, which is located at the corner of First Street. It was on this site in a house occupied by self-taught, unsuccessful lawyer Jonathan Jackson and his wife, Julia Neale Jackson, that Thomas was born on January 21, 1824. He was the third of four children born here, following brother Warren and sister Elizabeth. Records indicate that the baby was born *Thomas*. There

This plaque marks the site of Jackson's first home in downtown Clarksburg.

was no middle name or initial. During Jackson's stay at West Point, he started using *J.* as a middle initial, but it is only speculation that it stands for *Jonathan* in honor of his father.

The house apparently was small, as would befit a young country lawyer just getting started in his practice and in raising a family.

No photograph exists of Jackson's birthplace. Jackson had no memories of the house. If he had, they likely would have been sad, like most of his memories of childhood. Jackson was barely two years old when six-year-old Elizabeth and his father were stricken with typhoid fever in early March 1826. The day after Jonathan died, and 20 days after Elizabeth died, baby sister Laura was born in the house. Not long afterward, the family was forced to sell the house to settle Jonathan's debts. The Jacksons moved into a smaller house, the location of which remains unknown.

Life in the western expanses of Virginia must have been hard for the young widow and her three children, as Julia Jackson refused financial help from her family. Surviving details of the Jacksons' history indicate that she and the children were barely making it when

The grave of Jackson's father in Clarksburg, West Virginia

another lawyer came into her life. Blake B. Woodson was nearly old enough to be Julia's father when he married her in 1830. Thomas was five years old at the time. Not long afterward, Blake Woodson took his wife and his three stepchildren about 40 miles south of Clarksburg to a tiny community that would one day be called Ansted. There, he made a meager living as clerk of court.

Before you leave downtown Clarksburg, examine the statue of General Stonewall Jackson on the front lawn of the courthouse. It depicts a very aggressive-looking Jackson mounted on a horse. A full-sized copy of the statue stands in a city park in Charlottesville, Virginia. This is not the only instance of identical statues of Jackson. A statue depicting Jackson in a broad-brimmed hat (which he never wore) stands on the grounds of the West Virginia Capitol in Charleston; a copy of the same statue is located on the grounds of Virginia Military Institute in Lexington. These latter statues were crafted by Moses Ezekiel, once a student of Jackson's at V.M.I. and later one of the world's most famous sculptors working in bronze.

To see Jackson Historical Cemetery, drive east on Main Street for several blocks. Turn left on Monticello Avenue, drive one block to Pike Street, turn right, go eight blocks, and watch for the narrow

The statue of Jackson in his hometown

Cherry Street on the right. Follow Cherry Street to Linden Street, turn left, and park on Linden. Enter the cemetery and walk toward Pike Street. At the front of the cemetery are some poorly maintained signs pointing out the graves of Jackson's great-grandfather John (a Revolutionary War veteran); his great-grandmother Elizabeth; his father, Jonathan; and his older sister, Elizabeth.

It is recorded that Thomas Jackson visited this little cemetery only once after leaving Clarksburg at the age of five. There was little reason to return. Jackson had no direct memory of his father, as he was only two when the fever struck. The only influence Jonathan Jackson had on Thomas was in the act of dying, which created the melancholy mood that young Thomas observed in his mother as he grew up.

Still, in June 1855, Jackson came to the cemetery to visit the father and sister he never really knew. At that time, the graves were unmarked, but he told a distant cousin that he would buy stones. Since he never got around to buying a stone for his mother's grave, which he visited on the same trip, it is doubtful that the stones in the cemetery today are the same ones that Jackson wanted to order.

Weston/Jackson's Mill

Weston, the county seat of Lewis County, lies on US 33 about three miles west of I-79. It is 20 miles south of Jackson's hometown of Clarksburg.

Jackson's Mill, where Jackson spent his youth and teenage years before leaving for West Point, is about four miles northwest of Weston. Signs point the way out Main Avenue and CR 12. The restored mill is now part of the 4-H Conference Center. The mill generally opens for public tours in May. Call 304-269-5100 for information.

Weston was the first and largest town of which Jackson had childhood memories. He occasionally spent time in schools in town when a teacher was available. No schoolhouse attended by Jackson survives. The house where he took his entrance exam for the United States Military Academy was located at Main Avenue and First Street, where Citizens Bank now stands.

Resting in a virtually abandoned cemetery on the south side of

The grave of Gibson Jackson Butcher, the man who came home from West Point and whose place Jackson took

Weston is a man who had nothing to do with creating the legend of Stonewall Jackson but without whom there never would have been a Stonewall Jackson.

From downtown Weston where US 33 meets US 19, it is three blocks south to the **Y** intersection where Center and Main Avenues meet and where US 19 heads out of town. On a sloping ridge above this intersection is the now-abandoned Arnold Cemetery, or Old Hill Cemetery, which can be reached only on foot. There are parking spaces on US 19 Business heading into Weston. Walk up the steep slope toward a large tree and a metal shed. About 30 yards down from the shed and next to the fence-enclosed plot of the McClellan family is a single tombstone that is likely toppled from its original mount. It bears the faint inscription *G. J. Butcher*.

In January 1842, Congressman Samuel Lewis Hays, the representative for Lewis County, sent word to the voters back home that he had a slot to fill at the United States Military Academy in West Point, New York.

Weston was a long way from New York State. Indeed, it was a long way from Richmond, the capital of Virginia, where the United States Military Academy was a goal of many aristocratic boys living on the plantations. There was no aristocracy in Weston. But the people in the hills of western Virginia knew that West Point was emerging as one of the nation's best colleges. On top of that, an appointment meant that the government would educate one deserving boy for free, plus pay him a handsome salary of about $16 per month.

Four young men applied: 18-year-old Thomas Jackson, who may have never even met a soldier, since his life's experience had been limited to Jackson's Mill; Joseph Jackson Lightburn, Jackson's best friend, who lived about three miles from Jackson's Mill; Gibson Jackson Butcher, another teenage friend of Jackson's; and a fourth boy whose application was immediately rejected because he was under-age. For some reason—perhaps out of a growing religious faith—Lightburn withdrew his application, leaving only Butcher and Jackson to compete for the West Point slot. Butcher quickly emerged as the likely choice for the appointment, since he lived in Weston, which meant he had more opportunity for formal schooling than Jackson.

The exam was administered in a local hotel called the Bailey House, located where the bank now stands. Though he was not an orphan like Jackson, Butcher was illegitimate and had never known his father. Unfortunately for Jackson, Butcher was also brighter than he. Butcher was already serving as an apprentice clerk in the Lewis County Court. Jackson's only extracurricular experience—as important for the purpose of gaining admission to West Point back then as it is in college applications today—was serving as local constable, a job his uncle Cummins had procured. After the exams were graded, Butcher was the clear choice for the slot. Jackson had achieved excellent marks only in the math portion of the exam.

Butcher won the official appointment in April 1842. Jackson would have to find another way out of Jackson's Mill—or so he thought.

Butcher reported to West Point on June 3, 1842. Surprised at the discipline he would be expected to endure for the next four years, he spent less than a day at the academy before leaving on June 4. Incredibly, he departed without even bothering to tell the academy officers. Homegrown stories vary as to whether Butcher stopped by Jackson's Mill to tell his friend to apply in his place or whether he just went straight home. At any rate, when word got around Lewis County that Butcher was rejecting his West Point appointment, friends and acquaintances of the Jackson family swung into action to secure the appointment for Thomas.

As those friends gathered letters of recommendation for Thomas to give to Congressman Hays, Jackson was taken aside by some of the most learned men in the community and put into cram sessions to try to prepare him for the entrance exams that would be administered at the academy. More than two months had passed since Butcher's appointment, time that Jackson could have used to study for the final exams that were conducted prior to formal admission.

On June 17, 1842, just two weeks after Butcher rejected West Point, Jackson arrived in the Washington office of Congressman Hays to present his letters of recommendation. The surprised congressman was not even aware that Butcher had left, so he was more than willing to fill the slot with a boy who wanted to go to West Point. Within a day, Hays successfully appointed Jackson.

On June 19, 1842, Thomas Jackson stepped off a boat docked on the Hudson River and looked up at the school that would train him to become one of the most famous soldiers in American history.

Butcher stayed in Weston and eventually owned a tannery. He died in 1877 at the young age of 54. He appears to have been a simple man who knew what he wanted—and a military life was not it. Jackson had never expressed much interest in the military himself, but he knew that graduation from West Point would make him an educated man, give him the option of staying in the military if he wanted, and open up the world to him for whatever career he might want once he finished his military obligation.

Who knows what would have happened had Butcher stuck it out at West Point? Perhaps Jackson would have applied the following year. On the other hand, family stories say that Jackson was so disappointed in losing the appointment to Butcher that he might never have tried again. That means he would have likely settled into a career at his uncle's mills and that there never would have been a soldier called Stonewall. Though he did not know it at the time, Gibson Butcher played a major role in the history of the United States.

From downtown Weston, signs point the way out North Main Avenue toward Jackson's Mill, located on CR 12 about four and a half miles from town. The white mill standing on the grounds of the 4-H Conference Center beside the West Fork was built in 1841 by Cummins Jackson, Thomas's uncle and legal guardian. It replaced a mill that Cummins Jackson's father had built nearby that

Jackson's Mill

was threatened by the powerful current flowing down the creek.

This surviving mill was constructed of lumber from other Jackson sawmills. It is likely that Thomas, 17 years old at the time of construction, helped saw or place the beams in the mill and helped build the native-stone foundation. Jackson probably worked in the mill, but only briefly, as he went off to West Point the following year. From 1842 onward, Jackson was either in school, serving in the military, or paying brief visits to the family. He never held title to this property and never would have inherited it under any circumstances, as his father, Jonathan, had never helped his brothers around the mill.

The mill is the only surviving structure at Jackson's Mill that has a direct tie to Thomas. The houses in which he lived burned down years ago. The house where he lived just prior to going to West Point stood about 30 yards west of the mill. A large boulder with a historical marker embedded in it marks the spot. The cabins on the property were moved here in order to preserve them. They have no direct ties to Jackson.

About 200 yards west of the mill on the opposite side of the road is the Jackson family cemetery. It is surrounded by a wrought-iron fence. Buried here are John and Elizabeth Jackson (Thomas's

The site of the Jackson home across from the mill

grandparents) and several uncles and aunts. Missing from the cemetery is Cummins Jackson, Thomas's father's half-brother. It was
Cummins who agreed to take in Thomas and Laura after his sister-
in-law, Julia, pleaded that she and Blake Woodson were too poor to
continue raising the children.

Cummins came as close as anyone to being Jackson's father figure, though he would not have been anyone's choice for that role.
Though only 28 years old when he, speaking for all the family at
Jackson's Mill, agreed to take in the children, Cummins was already
a curmudgeon. A lifelong bachelor, he was kind toward his family
but harsh and scheming toward outsiders. The court records of Lewis
County from that period are filled with mentions of Cummins suing
someone over some minor property dispute, then being sued by them
over some other matter. He was not above cheating to get what he
wanted, nor above damming the creeks on his property and disrupt-
ing the water flow for his neighbors downstream.

Thomas Jackson picked up some of his uncle's bad traits, such as
cantankerousness and perhaps an occasional touch of dishonesty, if
the wartime testimony of some of his subordinates is to be believed.
Over the years, Thomas filed his own share of lawsuits and legal papers. During the war, he developed a reputation for preferring charges
against fellow officers for the slightest infraction.

The reason Cummins is not buried here with his father and brothers is that he went to California in the gold rush and died in 1849 in
Shasta County. His body was never returned.

Before leaving Jackson's Mill, walk along the West Fork, the little
creek that powers the mill. Just before Jackson drew his last breath
on May 10, 1863, in a little cabin about 25 miles from where he
had been wounded, witnesses said he opened his eyes wide, stared
at the ceiling, smiled, and then said, "Let us cross over the river
and rest in the shade of the trees." That statement still captures

the surroundings at Jackson's Mill, the only real childhood home Jackson ever had. It was here that the boy who was six when he arrived and 18 when he left for West Point found the happiness that had eluded him in Clarksburg and Ansted, the other two places he lived in childhood.

One other site associated with Jackson lies nearby. Drive west on CR 12 until it intersects CR 1 in less than two miles. Turn right, go 2.6 miles, and turn right on CR 8 (Broad Run Road). Just after turning, note the creek you will cross. Jackson was tossed by his horse into this creek one day on his way to Broad Run Baptist Church. Home on leave from West Point, he was dressed in his army uniform. Rather than skipping church or returning to Jackson's Mill, changing into dry clothes, and arriving late, Jackson went on to the service. The members of the congregation admired his determination, though they were distracted by the slow dripping of water from his uniform onto the floor.

Park and walk around Broad Run Baptist Church. Line up with the church bell in the back and walk about 200 feet into the cemetery. Look for a large Jackson family tombstone. A few feet in front of it is a modest obelisk for Joseph Andrew Jackson Lightburn,

Broad Run Baptist Church, where a soaked, embarrassed Jackson worshiped after falling into a nearby creek

Jackson's boyhood friend Joseph Lightburn, who later became a Union general, is buried at Broad Run Baptist Church.

Thomas's boyhood friend and later a Union general. Jackson often walked or rode to Lightburn's house, located about three miles through the woods from Jackson's Mill, to borrow books on religion, history, and philosophy.

As noted, no one knows why Lightburn took himself out of the running for the coveted West Point appointment in the winter of 1842. Of all the boys competing for the honor, Lightburn was probably the most military minded. Four years after dropping out of the West Point competition, he joined the United States Army as a volunteer in the Mexican War, during which he rose to the rank of sergeant. History does not record if he saw his old friend Thomas Jackson, who was serving as a commissioned second lieutenant in Mexico.

When the Civil War broke out 15 years later, Lightburn returned to the army and eventually worked his way up to a general's rank. He never ran into Jackson on the battlefield, since he served out west in Mississippi, Tennessee, and Georgia. It is doubtful that he and Jackson exchanged any letters during the war. It is more likely that after Thomas left Jackson's Mill for good in 1846, he drifted away from his friend.

Lightburn's family was touched by the war. His brother joined the Confederate forces and was captured. Family tradition says that Union general Lightburn did what he could to take care of his imprisoned brother, including smuggling him gold coins so he could buy extra food from the prison guards.

In 1868, Jackson's old friend became an ordained minister. He preached for many years at this church. Oddly, his tombstone mentions his military service but not his religious service.

Ansted

This town is located on US 60 about six miles west of the intersection with US 19 and about six miles north of Fayetteville. Look for a Rite Aid pharmacy in the downtown area. Turn north down an unmarked road that has a sign pointing to Westlake Cemetery. In this little cemetery rest the mortal remains of Julia Neale Jackson Woodson, Thomas Jackson's mother. Drive to the first road leading left into the cemetery and park. Walk diagonally up a steep hill into the cemetery. Look for a large metal sign announcing the Woodson grave.

If the future general had only dim memories of his life in Clarksburg as a toddler and young child, he retained terrible memories of his short stay as a boy on a farm near Ansted. At an age when others were playing in the woods or splashing in streams, Thomas was listening to his stepfather tell his mother that she had to give up all three of her children—Warren, 10, Thomas, seven, and Laura, five.

The reason was all too familiar to Julia. She had picked the wrong man to marry. Just as Jonathan Jackson had been a poor lawyer who never developed a reputation for knowing—or even following—the law, Blake Woodson was a poor lawyer who never developed a reputation for working very hard at anything. When Julia's health began failing, Woodson convinced her that the best thing to do was to parcel her children out to relatives.

Warren went to Parkersburg to live with Julia's parents, while Thomas and Laura were to live with Jonathan Jackson's brothers at Jackson's Mill, about 85 miles north of Ansted and 20 miles south of Clarksburg, their hometown. It is doubtful that young Thomas had even met his uncles before Blake Woodson sent a short letter telling them to come pick up the children before he sent them to an orphanage.

Anna Morrison Jackson, the general's second wife, later wrote in her biography of him that Thomas had a clear memory of his mother's farewell on that occasion. She ran out to hug him one last time as he mounted a horse.

Jackson saw his mother again just three months later, but the reunion was not happy. Sensing that she was finally dying of tuberculosis, Julia sent word to Jackson's Mill for the children to come. An elderly slave called Uncle Robinson brought them down to Ansted for a deathbed meeting, then returned them to Jackson's Mill before Julia died in December 1831.

The next time Jackson was in Ansted—and the only occasion he visited this cemetery—was in June 1855, when he was 31 years old and mourning the death of his first wife, Ellie, who had passed away while giving birth in October 1854. Though Ellie had died nearly nine months earlier, Jackson remained in mourning as the fall school term approached. Apparently in an attempt to reconnect with his roots, sad as they were, Jackson spent the summer wandering western Virginia. In addition to visiting his sister and her family in Beverly, other relatives in Clarksburg, and the home of his youth at Jackson's Mill, he went to Parkersburg to visit his uncle's family. If the time line and the description of the trip in Jackson's letters are accurate, he chose not to visit Ansted when he was relatively close by in Clarksburg and Jackson's Mill. Instead, he visited his uncle and aunt in Parkersburg, then backtracked to Ansted. It almost seems that Jackson was steeling himself to finally visit his mother's grave. Or maybe he was talked into going by his uncle and aunt.

The visit was heartbreaking. When Jackson stopped in tiny Ansted, he found one man who claimed to know where his mother had been buried nearly 25 years earlier. The man pointed out a bare patch of

The grave of Jackson's mother in Ansted, West Virginia

ground without a tombstone. Woodson had died a year and a half after Julia, having married another woman. Still poor at his death, it is doubtful that Woodson had the money to mark Julia's grave.

Jackson had promised his cousin to mark his father's grave in Clarksburg. It is unknown whether he promised himself to mark his mother's grave here. For reasons unknown, he never erected either stone, even though he spent the middle and late 1850s accumulating considerable wealth for a college professor.

Perhaps the reason Jackson never returned to Ansted or Clarksburg was that after his marriage to Anna Morrison in the summer of 1857, the lonely little orphan who had lost his first love and first child finally found the happiness that had always eluded him. Perhaps a journey back to those two sad little cemeteries would have only reminded him of his lost youth.

It was several years after the war that an officer of the Stonewall Brigade journeyed to Ansted and erected the stone that now rests over Julia Neale Jackson Woodson.

Buckhannon

This town, the site of Heavner Cemetery, lies at the intersection of WV 20 and US 33 about 25 miles west of Elkins.

Laura Jackson Arnold, Thomas's estranged sister, divorced in 1870. Divorce was rare in rural Virginia in those days. She subsequently drifted among hospitals and the homes of her children. She finally died in 1911 at the age of 85, some 48 years after her brother.

The grave of Laura Jackson Arnold, Jackson's sister, in Buckhannon

To visit her grave, take the Morton Avenue (CR 134) exit off US 33 outside Buckhannon. Follow Morton Avenue north under US 33. As the road curves, you will see an entrance to Heavner Cemetery. Ignore this first entrance. As the road continues to curve, tombstones will appear on both sides of the road. Take the next left into the cemetery. Drive uphill about 100 yards. Stop at the large tombstone marked *Arnold*. Laura lies under the fourth stone away from the road. The tombstone has a scroll atop it.

Beverly

This small town is located on US 219/US 250 south of Elkins. Laura Jackson Arnold, Thomas's sister, lived in the much-modified red-brick house at the corner of Main Street and the Staunton-Parkersburg Turnpike. A historical marker describes the house and the general's visits to it. The house is private. Please do not trespass.

Even without its connection to the Jackson family, Beverly would be a significant Civil War town. The Battle of Rich Mountain, fought just west of the village in June 1861, was the first significant battle of the war. It was a Union victory, giving hope to the Federals that the war would be over quickly. The site of the battle is preserved today.

Stonewall Jackson's association with the town is a sad one. Few family stories are more tragic than those of orphaned children who help each other grow up, then break apart as adults. That happened to Jackson and his sister Laura, born in Clarksburg just two years after Thomas. For the first 34 years of Thomas's life, they were close. They grew up together at Jackson's Mill, then kept in contact by letter when Thomas fought the loneliness of West Point. The bond did not end when Laura married Jonathan Arnold and moved to Beverly. Thomas and Laura counseled each other on everything from family matters to business to religion to where the best healing springs were located. Laura loved her brother so much that she named her son Thomas Jackson Arnold. Thomas worshiped his nephew.

As might be expected in any relationship, brother and sister sometimes disagreed. The two often argued in letters about the existence of God. Though his introduction to formal religion as a child was spotty, Jackson the West Point cadet and young lieutenant began a search for a religion to which he could devote himself. At the same time he was becoming more spiritual, his sister was losing faith that there even was a God, thanks to bouts of poor health and to depression over the illness of her own daughter.

"For my part, I am willing to go hence when it shall be his great will to terminate my earthly career. I should regret to leave you unconverted, but his will and not mine be done," Jackson wrote Laura from Fort Hamilton, New York, in 1849.

Jackson never could bring his sister to religion. That may have

Laura Jackson Arnold's house in Beverly, West Virginia

played a part in why he did not invite her to either of his weddings, choosing instead to take his brides to see her in Beverly as they passed through on their honeymoons. On several occasions in the 1850s, Jackson, sometimes alone and sometimes with his first or second wife, visited his sister here.

When the war came along in 1861, the brother and sister who had clung to each other through childhood allowed politics to break them apart. Jackson chose to follow his native Virginia out of the Union, while Laura defied both her brother and—more remarkably— her husband to become a Unionist. Without a final farewell, the two seem to have simply stopped writing to each other.

For whatever reason, Laura could not just allow her brother to become part of her past. As Jackson grew more famous, Laura began to spread rumors that he had somehow cheated on his West Point entrance exams and had not been deserving of the slot he had won 19 years earlier.

More disturbingly, she openly defied her pro-Confederate neighbors and nursed wounded Union soldiers in her home. It was not long before rumors started circulating in Beverly that she was doing more than just tending to those soldiers' healing. Whispers began that Laura was also consorting with Union officers, stories that were never proved but that she did not indignantly and publicly deny either. The rumors grew so great that her husband finally left her, though the divorce did not become final until several years after the war.

For his part, Jackson rarely even mentioned his sister during the war. Visitors were often reluctant to bring him news from that part of the state, lest they set off the famous Jackson temper.

Even after Jackson was killed in May 1863, Laura did not express any regrets about the death of the brother who had helped her grow up as an orphan child. She made no effort to attend any of the many memorial services held in his honor, nor did she attend the large funeral service in Lexington, only a few days' ride from Beverly. She apparently never met Julia, the niece named for her own mother, though Anna (Jackson's second wife) wrote her during the war to inform her of the baby's birth, in an attempt to bring Laura back into contact with the family.

Romney

Romney is on US 50 about 40 miles west of Winchester, Virginia, the site of Stonewall Jackson's headquarters. The Romney house that Jackson and then his subordinate general, William Wing Loring, occupied as a headquarters is about 0.2 mile east of the intersection with WV 28. It has a historical marker but is a private dwelling. It was from this house that a letter was sent that almost ended Jackson's career.

Romney sits less than a mile from the South Branch of the Potomac River, which is barely more than a stream at this point. It was not 40 miles from important Union-held towns like Hancock and Cumberland, Maryland. A determined Union force operating from any or all three of those towns—Romney, Hancock, and Cumberland—could swoop down on Winchester, the principal town at the head of the Shenandoah Valley. In Jackson's mind, Romney was a Union beachhead with a force that would always be waiting for him to leave Winchester, his center of operations going into the winter of 1861-62.

But Jackson also noticed something else about Romney. The force stationed there was relatively small (as were those in Hancock and Cumberland). The Union strategy at that time was to keep a presence in several towns, so as to be able to raid the Confederate side of the Potomac, then return. Jackson reasoned that he might be able to attack each town and destroy the garrisons before they had a chance to unite against him. At the very least, he could cut off the Romney garrison before it could get back across the Potomac.

In late November 1861, Jackson got permission to launch a peremptory attack on the Union forces along the Potomac River in Maryland, then to wipe out the garrison in Romney. He thought his force was too weak for such a venture, so he asked that General William Loring's Army of the Northwest be ordered to cooperate in the movement. Loring's army, which had already participated in both the abortive Cheat Mountain and Sewell Mountain campaigns a few months earlier under Lee, was still a couple of hundred miles away.

Loring's men had barely made it to Winchester in late December 1861 when Jackson told them to prepare to move on Romney. The footsore, sick, hungry, and exhausted troops thought Jackson was insane to ask them to march still more miles without any rest, but Loring had no choice but to put his men into motion.

The Romney campaign started on January 1, 1862. Temperatures were in the 50s. Of the four brigades of Confederates participating, three were under the direct command of Loring and only one—the Stonewall Brigade—was under Jackson. While Loring was supposed to be "supporting" Jackson, Jackson thought of himself as being in command of the entire operation.

Within hours of the time the Confederates left Winchester, the weather turned cold and it started snowing. The men spent the night just eight miles outside Winchester in Pughtown (now Gainesboro). They covered just seven miles the next day. Loring's men were several miles short of Unger's Store when Jackson sent word for them to come up immediately. Most of the troops had not eaten a hot meal for two days. Some were openly questioning Jackson's sanity in pushing them so close to exhaustion. Even Jackson's own commanders began to doubt him. General Richard Garnett was rebuked by Jackson for allowing the men of the Stonewall Brigade, Jackson's former brigade, to cook their rations.

The Confederates captured the town of Berkeley Springs (or Bath) on January 4.

The following day, Jackson started to retrace his steps to Unger's Store in a snowstorm. His force was there for several days when word came that Romney had been abandoned without a fight.

On January 14, 1862, Jackson rode into Romney at the head of the Stonewall Brigade. Loring's men had hardly stumbled in after them before Jackson began planning an attack still farther westward. Loring finally put his foot down and convinced Jackson that his troops were too tired and sick to continue.

Five days later, Jackson and the Stonewall Brigade marched out of Romney, leaving Loring and his men in an exposed position; they were sitting ducks for Federal forces attacking from Hancock, Cumberland, or both. That was the last straw for Loring's officers. While Jackson and his Stonewall Brigade "pets" (as Loring's men called them) would be safe and sound in Winchester, Loring and his broken-down, sick soldiers, who had been marching continually since

*Jackson's headquarters in Romney, where his
subordinate officers rebelled against him*

August, would be sacrificial lambs for the Federals or so they thought.

Six days after Jackson left, almost all of Loring's officers came to him at his headquarters in Romney with a letter protesting that Jackson had subjected the men to "terrible exposure and suffering on this expedition [that] can never be known to those who did not participate in it." The letter continued, "We regard Romney as a place difficult to hold, and of no strategical importance after it is held." A later portion read, "When we left Winchester, a very large portion of your army, with the benefit of a short furlough, would have enlisted for the war, but now, with the present prospect before them, we doubt if a single man would re-enlist. But if they are yet removed to a position where their spirits could be revived, many, we think, will go for the war. In view of all these considerations and many others that may be presented, we ask that you present the condition of your command to the War Department, and earnestly ask that it may be ordered to some more favorable position."

The letter was asking Loring to go over Jackson's head to Secretary of War Judah P. Benjamin to get the troops out of Romney. Loring forwarded the letter to Jackson, per military protocol. Jackson signed it and forwarded it to Richmond with the notation, "Respectfully forwarded, but disapproved."

Within days of getting the letter, Benjamin ordered Jackson to bring Loring's troops out of Romney.

The same day he received that letter from Benjamin at his headquarters in Winchester, Jackson wrote out a letter of resignation to protest Benjamin's interference in his command decisions. When the letter arrived in Richmond, Jackson's friends, including the governor of Virginia, stormed to Benjamin's and Jefferson Davis's offices to demand that they apologize to Jackson. A direct apology was never made, but Jackson's friends secured assurances that no more politicians would interfere in his military decisions. Jackson withdrew the resignation letter, which had asked that he be assigned back to his professorship at V.M.I.

Berkeley Springs

This town is located at the junction of US 522 and WV 9 about 40 miles northeast of Romney and about 40 miles north of Winchester, Virginia. You can contact Berkeley Springs State Park at 304-258-2711 for information on taking a mineral-water bath and getting a massage at the same springs captured—and probably bathed in—by Jackson.

Jackson's roundabout attack route from Winchester, Virginia, to Romney in January 1862 took him first to Gainesboro, Unger, and Berkeley Springs, all towns that still exist along US 522 heading out of Winchester. The most prominent landmark on the attack route is

Berkeley Springs State Park

what is now Berkeley Springs State Park in downtown Bath. The oldest
state park in the nation, it is located in a town that claims to have
more licensed massage therapists than lawyers.

On January 3, 1862, Jackson prepared to attack Bath (now called
Berkeley Springs, though the town has never officially changed its
name). Jackson and General William Loring had a confrontation just
south of the town after Jackson deployed Loring's troops without
Loring issuing the order. The actual attack was botched. Most of the
Union garrison Jackson had counted on capturing escaped across the
Potomac to Hancock, Maryland. A frustrated Jackson shelled
Hancock—one of several unauthorized attacks on Union territory
he would make in his career.

That evening, Jackson did what some commanders consider un-
pardonable—he favored the Stonewall Brigade over other troops in
his command. While his personal brigade was quartered inside some
buildings in downtown Bath, Loring's men—including other Virginia

regiments—were left to fend for themselves in the open.

The buildings where Jackson quartered his men were part of Strother's Berkeley Hotel. Normally, Jackson would have been reluctant to take over private property, but David Hunter Strother, son of the hotel's builder, was a Union officer. Jackson had no problem using the property of a Virginian who had abandoned his state loyalties. David Strother was famous in his own right as an artist and correspondent for *Harper's Weekly*, working under the pseudonym Porte Crayon. Visitors will find no trace of Strother's Berkeley Hotel today, as it burned in 1898. It was located around what is now Berkeley Springs State Park.

While no written record exists that Jackson took a bath in the springs during his one-night occupation of Bath, he almost certainly did. The air may have been freezing, but the water was a constant 74 degrees and filled with the minerals Jackson believed to be beneficial to his health. He had visited health spas for 13 years in New York State, Massachusetts, and Virginia. There is every reason to suspect he visited one in the town he had just captured.

Falling Waters

The small community of Falling Waters, a collection of RV camps and weekend river houses today, was the place where Jackson was baptized by fire in early July 1861. Located about 10 miles north of Martinsburg on US 11, the Falling Waters battlefield is unmarked but likely begins at the road signs announcing the unincorporated community. The Potomac River makes a bend to the west here. The ford at Falling Waters was recognized by both sides.

No man in the Confederate army was more eager to fight the Federals than Colonel Thomas Jackson. Chastised once by his superiors in April 1861 for illegally fortifying Maryland Heights across from Harpers Ferry, Jackson had since received a second lecture from his superior, Joseph Johnston, about his eagerness to fight. Johnston feared that Jackson would get into a running battle with the Federals along the Valley Turnpike (today's US 11) and would pursue them back into Maryland. That would lead to a political crisis, as the Confederate government in Richmond was trying to woo slaveholding Maryland into the Confederacy. It would not do for the army of one Southern state to invade another.

Jackson chafed under the orders that he was to fall back if the Federals approached his camp at Martinsburg "in force." Long before Lee or President Davis even thought about invading the North, Jackson was already advocating it to a few close friends. He believed a lightning fast invasion of the North would prove to the Federal government that the South was serious about leaving the Union, and that the Confederates would deal with any force on their borders, even if that force was still in the North.

On the morning of July 2, 1861, Jackson got word that troops under Union general Robert Patterson had crossed the Potomac and were making their way south toward Martinsburg. Jackson mobilized about half his 2,300-man brigade and started marching north from Camp Stephens along the turnpike. He also took Colonel William Pendleton's four-gun battery—whose cannons were nicknamed Matthew, Mark, Luke, and John, in mocking honor of Pendleton's peacetime job as an Episcopal minister.

One of Jackson's regiments met the strong Federal force not far south of Falling Waters. It immediately found itself in trouble, as the Federals had it heavily outnumbered. Pendleton helped by aiming one of his six-pounders down the road. Just before firing, the minister said—or legend has him saying—"May the Lord have mercy on their souls. Fire!"

Jackson began a slow retreat back toward Martinsburg. At some point along the road—perhaps three miles south of Falling Waters— he paused to write a short report to Johnston concerning the ongoing action. A cannonball slammed into a nearby tree, showering Jackson with bark. He never stopped writing. It was the first of several close calls Jackson had during the war. His calmness came from his belief that his time to die had already been predetermined by the Lord and that there was nothing he could do to change his fate.

Jackson retreated through Martinsburg, following his strict orders that he not bring on a general engagement. He reached the small town of Darksville, where he wrote his first battle report of the war. He had lost no men known killed, but 13 were missing and might have been left dead on the battlefield. He also lost 12 wounded. The Federals suffered at least 10 killed by their own accounting, 18 wounded, and at least 50 captured by a bold Jackson flanking maneuver—something that would make him famous in less than two years.

It is hard to classify this first action of Jackson's. It was not a battle; it was barely even a skirmish. Jackson withdrew from the battlefield, since his scouting force numbered only 300 or so against 3,000. That meant it was technically a defeat, usually designated when one side leaves the battlefield to the other. Yet it really was not a defeat, since Jackson inflicted more damage on the Federals than they inflicted on him, and since his orders were to retreat in the face of the enemy and not bring on a major engagement. Jackson kept his men moving to the rear toward safety, but he fought stubbornly, making the Federals pay for the ground they gained.

Coming so soon after the June 3, 1861, defeat at Philippi, Virginia, where Confederate troops ran from the battle, the little fight at Falling Waters seemed to mean more than it really did. But the South did come out ahead when the troops killed, wounded, and captured, were counted, though the Confederate forces were vastly outnumbered.

Falling Waters would hardly be remembered three weeks later, after First Manassas, yet it served to introduce the South to the fighting abilities of Colonel Thomas Jackson. His commanders already knew he could train men. Now, they had evidence he could follow orders—even orders he did not like or agree with—and that he could command men to follow the complex maneuvers they had been practicing in their training camps.

Jackson had proven himself for the first time.

A small battle took place on the Maryland side of the river opposite Falling Waters on July 14, 1863. It resulted in the mortal wounding of Confederate general James Johnston Pettigrew. Pettigrew was taken to the Boyd House in Bunker Hill, Jackson's September 1862 headquarters, where he died.

Martinsburg

Martinsburg is on US 11 in northeast West Virginia.

Though Jackson probably never visited it, the childhood home of Confederate spy Belle Boyd is located at 126 East Race Street in Martinsburg. Call 304-267-4713 for information about this fine little museum tracing the famous woman's life. Depending on which historical account you read, Jackson never met Boyd or personally thanked her for her role in helping capture Front Royal in May 1862.

It was what happened at the railroad roundhouses at 229 East Martin Street in downtown Martinsburg that helped develop Stonewall Jackson's reputation for doing the impossible. The station house that existed at the time still stands on the corner as a restored office building. The original roundhouses were destroyed by the Confederates during the war, but the roundhouse across the tracks was rebuilt in 1866 on the same ground and in the same style as the original.

Colonel Thomas Jackson arrived in Martinsburg in June 1861 with distasteful orders from his superior, General Joseph Johnston, to destroy the roundhouses, locomotives, and rolling stock kept there by the Baltimore & Ohio Railroad. Jackson was torn by the orders. He thought the destruction of private property, particularly that located in his native state, to be wasteful. He was so conscious of hurting civilians that he sometimes punished his own men for tearing down wooden fences to make campfires.

Ignoring the anger of Martinsburg's townspeople, most of whom harbored Unionist leanings, Jackson's men first destroyed the roundhouses and the downtown tracks. They were in the process of wrecking several dozen locomotives and railroad cars when Jackson got an

The B & O roundhouses in Martinsburg were rebuilt after Jackson wrecked them.

inspiration—a wild one, to be sure. He decided to run it by some locomotive engineers.

Salvaging 13 locomotives from the scrap heap he had just created, Jackson had the engines repaired and fitted with wooden wheels. He then hitched horse teams to them and pulled them nearly 40 miles to Strasburg, Virginia, where they were transferred to another railroad that eventually took them to Richmond, where they were repaired.

It was the first time that Jackson thought about the strategic value fast transportation offered his troops. He followed this effort just one month later by boarding his men on trains for First Manassas.

Jackson camped and trained his men at Camp Stephens, located about four miles north of Martinsburg along the Valley Turnpike (now US 11). There is no sign of the camp today.

It was while in this area on July 2, 1861, that Jackson got his first taste of combat since 1847. It came near the entrance of a stream into the Potomac River called Falling Waters.

Darksville

This unincorporated village is located on US 11 three miles north of Bunker Hill. A few of the houses here look old enough to have been standing at the time Jackson made his brief visit.

Jackson spent a few days in the village of Darksville in early July 1861 after fighting his first skirmish of the war on July 2. That action took place at Falling Waters, located about 15 miles to the north.

Darksville was where Jackson wrote his first battle report and where General Joseph Johnston came to review Jackson's troops after their slow, fighting retreat back through Martinsburg to this spot. Though the skirmish was inconsequential—almost meaningless for both sides—the South considered it a minor victory. There had been so little fighting up until Falling Waters that the South immediately took to Colonel Thomas Jackson as one of its first heroes. This was three weeks before he acquired his famous nickname. One of General Johnston's aides complained that it seemed the men ignored the general in favor of staring at their colonel.

For his part, Johnston wanted to do what he could to praise the Confederate commander, Jackson. From Darksville, he wrote a report to Lee urging that Colonel Jackson be promoted to general. Though the recommendation to appoint Jackson a brigadier general was approved by the Confederate Congress on July 3, while Jackson was in Darksville, Jackson did not receive notice of his promotion until five days later, when he had returned to Winchester. His short note from Lee read, "My dear general, I have the pleasure of sending you a commission of brigadier general in the Provisional Army, and to feel that you merit it. May your advancement increase your usefulness to the state."

Bunker Hill

The small community of Bunker Hill lies about eight miles south of Martinsburg on US 11. The Boyd House, a bed-and-breakfast dedicated to weddings, is located here. Just to the east

The front yard of the Boyd House in Bunker Hill was the site of a historic—and decidedly unfruitful—meeting among Jackson, Lee, and Ambrose Powell Hill.

Dating back to their West Point days of 1842-46, Jackson and Hill disliked each other. Jackson was a rough-hewn, poorly educated boy from the mountains of western Virginia. Hill was an aristocrat from Culpeper who looked down his nose at poor boys like Jackson. This culture clash between the two opened wounds that had not healed 19 years later, when the two men met on the same side of the battlefield.

When the war started, Jackson's star ascended faster than Hill's. Jackson won early favor by organizing and training troops at Harpers Ferry. A few months later, he earned fame in the first major battle, First Manassas, where Hill was held in reserve. By contrast, in the first major campaign of the Army of Northern Virginia, the Seven Days, Hill proved to be impatient and showed a tendency to act without direct orders. His personality was a mixture of traits such as aggressiveness, which can be good in a general, and impetuousness, which can be bad. Many of Hill's men died because of his impatience. Time and time again, Hill proved himself a good on-field fighting general like Jackson, but not a thinking general like Jackson was becoming. Assigned to Jackson's corps, Hill grinned and bore it, content for the moment to build his Light Division, so named because it was understrength in numbers but was still expected to perform the role of a division.

It was while in Virginia on the way toward invading the North that two decades of animosity finally boiled over. On September 4, 1862, Jackson ordered his corps into the road just north of Dranesville. The troops were to begin a long day's march that would end with their crossing the Potomac River into Maryland. The previous evening, Jackson had instructed his generals to have their divisions on the road early in the morning. As he rode to the head of what he expected to be a column, he found much of Hill's Light Division still cooking breakfast instead of forming into marching ranks. Hill was nowhere to be found. When Jackson rode to the head of Hill's column, he still found no Hill. At that point, he noted that the lead portion of the column had been marching for 50 minutes. By regulations, and by his precise instructions the previous night, the column should have stopped for a 10-minute break. When its general did not halt it, Jackson himself ordered the break, a breach of military etiquette, since Jackson was not the brigade's direct commander.

Within a few minutes, Hill, who had been riding well in advance of the column, came storming back. He demanded that the brigadier tell him the reason the column was stopped. The brigadier, Edward Thomas, was thus caught in a difficult spot. His commanding general, Jackson, had already embarrassed him by giving the men a direct order to stop marching. Now, his immediate superior, Hill, was demanding to know who had issued that order.

When Thomas explained what had happened, an infuriated Hill rode up to Jackson, pulled out his sword by the hilt, and offered it to Jackson, saying, "I submit my resignation!"

Jackson, resisting the urge to get into a shouting match with one of his generals, quietly said, "General Hill, consider yourself under arrest for disobedience of orders."

Jackson's arrest of Hill was astonishing. Lee's army was on its way into Maryland—dangerous, never-before-visited territory—and two of his top generals were arguing over a 10-minute rest period. Hill, knowing his division was late in starting the march, likely was trying to make up for lost ground by skipping the first rest period, thinking that would be what Jackson wanted. But Jackson was a stickler for army regulations, even if they did not always make sense. If the regulations demanded a 10-minute rest after marching 50 minutes, and particularly if he had ordered that rest, he expected those orders to be carried out.

Hill retook command of the Light Division as battle neared during the Sharpsburg Campaign 10 days later, but Jackson never withdrew the charges. Hill subsequently demanded through Lee that Jackson admit he was wrong in arresting him.

Jackson was not willing to do that. He told Lee that Hill had disobeyed orders and had been arrested in response. What Jackson would do, he told Lee, was let the matter drop, since Hill had learned his lesson that orders were orders.

Letting the matter drop was not what Hill had in mind. He had been arrested, and Jackson had not apologized or withdrawn the charges. Hill demanded a full-fledged court of inquiry to investigate the charge that he had not stopped his men's marching for 10 minutes.

Three weeks after Sharpsburg, Lee himself rode to Jackson's headquarters to mediate the dispute. The three generals—the commander of the entire army, the commander of half the army, and a division commander—went into a tent in the front yard of the Boyd House to iron out a dispute over marching—or rather not marching—for 10 minutes. Though the details of what the three said to each other in the tent have been lost to history, it was an obviously frustrated Lee who emerged. Neither Jackson nor Hill was willing to bend on what they perceived as their principles. For the eight months until

*The Boyd House in Bunker Hill, Jackson's
headquarters after Sharpsburg*

Jackson's death, the two men spoke only formally to each other, and no more than was necessary. Hill followed his orders from Jackson exactly as they were given, offering no opinions and no options to be considered.

This front yard thus saw Jackson's pettiness. It also saw his playfulness.

General James Ewell Brown Stuart, commander of the Confederate cavalry, would seem on the surface to be an unusual friend for Stonewall Jackson. Jackson was normally serious, whereas Stuart did not know the meaning of the word. Being serious would have cut into the fun he was having fighting the war. While Jackson could not carry a tune in a bucket, Stuart actively recruited staff members who could play instruments around his tent. While Jackson never looked at another woman, Stuart loved nothing more than flirting with admiring ladies—the more the better.

Yet Jackson liked Stuart. For all his frivolity, Stuart was a deeply religious man who believed, much like Jackson, that battles were decided by the will of God more than by accurate musket and cannon fire. And Stuart obeyed orders, another trait that Jackson admired.

It was while Jackson was camped in this yard that Stuart rode up late one night coming back from a patrol. Rather than waking Jackson to report, Stuart simply slipped into Jackson's tent, lay down beside his commander, and went to sleep. Such "spooning" and sharing blankets were quite common in those days.

The next day, Stuart emerged from the tent to find Jackson and the rest of his staff warming themselves by the fire. Stuart boomed out, "Good morning, General Jackson!"

Jackson's eyes bore a hole through Stuart, which told Stuart that the previous night's foray into Jackson's tent had not gone entirely well.

"General Stuart. I am always glad to see you here. You might select better hours sometimes, and general, you must not get into my bed with your boots and spurs on and ride me around like a cavalry horse all night!"

Stuart, always the joker, was finally the victim of a verbal joust at the hands of the dour, thought-to-be humorless Jackson.

Not long afterward, Stuart got his chance at revenge, again at Jackson's headquarters at the Boyd House. Stuart, always a fashion plate with his tailored uniforms, plumed hats, and crimson-lined capes, often made fun of Jackson's old, worn V.M.I. uniform, which had faded from its once-bright blue after two years of service in the sun.

Without Jackson's knowledge, and guessing at his measurements, Stuart ordered a new, gray general's coat from a Richmond tailor. It had gold braid fit for any dapper general, which Jackson most certainly was not.

When a Stuart aide delivered the coat, Jackson was surprised and unsure what he was supposed to do with it, other than keep it as a souvenir. The aide insisted that Stuart expected Jackson to wear the coat and would be insulted if Jackson did not.

Incredible as it may sound to people used to thinking of Jackson as a sober, serious man, he put on the coat and even twirled as if he were putting on an impromptu fashion show. Jackson wore the coat on occasion but almost always took the field in his plain, faded V.M.I. coat and plain, faded United States Army forage hat with the bill pulled low over his eyes.

The fancy gift coat from Stuart can be seen in the April 1863 photograph of Jackson showing him in profile.

Shepherdstown

Located at the intersection of WV 480, WV 34, and WV 45, Shepherdstown is on the south bank of the Potomac River just across from Maryland.

Boteler's Ford, used by Jackson to reach and then retreat from Sharpsburg in September 1862, is two miles south of downtown. Follow West German Street (CR17) east out of town until it runs alongside the Potomac. Watch for the historical markers indicating a shallow spot in the river about 300 yards wide. This site was also known as Pack Horse Ford.

Elmwood Cemetery is located on Duke Street less than half a mile from the intersection of WV 480 and WV 45.

The people of Shepherdstown likely were not thrilled to see Jackson in early June 1861 when he made his first visit. He was under orders to burn the bridge over the Potomac to keep it from being used by the Federals as part of an invasion route into upper Virginia.

The remains of the stone bridge supports can be seen on the east side of the modern bridge.

Jackson returned to the area in September 1862 to Boteler's Ford, named after the family of Alexander Boteler, the man credited with pushing the Confederate government to give Jackson his first chance at command at Harpers Ferry. The ford, about hip deep under normal conditions, was the easiest access route from Harpers Ferry to Sharpsburg. It was used by Jackson after he captured Harpers Ferry on September 15, 1862. The all-night 17-mile march from Harpers Ferry to the ford greatly taxed Jackson's men, but they held their predawn marching formation as they crossed into Maryland, an invasion of the North that Jackson had been advocating since April 1861. The march was so fast that estimates have suggested as many as half the troops had to drop out of formation to rest. It was actually the third time in the span of a few days that Jackson had crossed the Potomac. He had first entered Maryland at White's Ford north of Leesburg, Virginia, then come back into Virginia from Williamsport, Maryland.

On September 18, three days after the march from Harpers Ferry, the once-joyous army splashed back across the ford again, in retreat after the Battle of Sharpsburg. The ranks had been tight going into Maryland, but they were ragged coming back into Virginia. Jackson sat astride his horse in the middle of the river watching the mass of humanity crowd past. He finally asked his quartermaster, John Harman, to straighten out the traffic jam before all order was lost.

By the morning of September 19, most of the army had crossed the river. To buy time and to make sure that the Union army did not follow too closely, Lee stationed 40 cannons along the Virginia bluffs looking down on the river.

That night, a sizable Federal force crossed the Potomac upriver from this spot, out of sight of the guarding Confederates. General

William Pendleton, commanding the cannons, allowed the Federal force to surprise him. He panicked, rushing to Lee's headquarters and erroneously reporting that the Federals had captured all of the reserve cannons.

Jackson ordered a brigade from A. P. Hill's division back to the river. Jackson himself rode there to direct the counterattack. The Federal force was not as strong as expected and was made up mostly of inexperienced soldiers. Hill's men made short work of them. Many of the 200 Federal deaths occurred when the panicked men rushed back into the river and drowned as they fell into deep holes and were pulled down by their equipment, or when they were wounded and found themselves unable to swim.

The Battle of Boteler's Ford has remained controversial through the years. The Reverend Pendleton, a friend of Lee's, had endangered the entire Army of Northern Virginia by his improper guarding of the river crossing, yet Lee did not ask for his resignation. Jackson's supporters claimed that he alone saved the army with his quick assignment of Hill to the river. Those supporters ignored the whole erroneous premise of Pendleton's report—namely, that the Federals had captured 40 Confederate cannons. In actuality, they had captured only four, and the number of Federals on the Virginia side of the river was never more than a few hundred. Indeed, it was George McClellan's reluctance to launch a major attack on Lee that led to his firing by President Abraham Lincoln.

If you care to see the graves of a couple of men who played prominent roles in Jackson's life, visit Elmwood Cemetery in Shepherdstown.

After turning into the cemetery, stop at the box and pick up a map of the famous graves. Continue past the Confederate cemetery on the right and stop about halfway up the hill. On the left next to the road is the grave of Alexander Boteler.

Boteler was one of the many powerful friends that Jackson courted and kept as he gained prominence. Though often considered shy, Jackson had learned from his uncle Cummins the ability to recognize powerful political friends and to keep them in his company. Boteler had briefly served in the United States Congress and was a Confederate congressman when he first started supporting Jackson, since Jackson was the first line of defense in his native area of Virginia. It was Boteler who, rather than submit to political interference from Secretary of War Judah P. Benjamin, stormed into the office of President Jefferson Davis in January 1862 with the news that Jackson had submitted his resignation from the army. Boteler then stormed over to the office of Governor John Letcher, another Jackson friend from Lexington. Together, the two men shamed Davis and Benjamin into indirectly apologizing to Jackson and assuring him that they would not interfere with his battlefield decisions again. Recognizing the value of friends in high places, Jackson made Boteler an adviser on his staff, though Boteler spent most of his time in Richmond.

During a break one day in July 1862, Boteler noticed Jackson leaning on a fence rail. Boteler quickly sketched the general from

the left rear, emphasizing what would become a Jackson trademark—an old army fatigue cap pulled down so low over his forehead that it almost hid his eyes. Jackson turned and noticed what Boteler was doing. He came over

Alexander Boteler's grave in Shepherdstown

and took the sketch pad from the congressman. Boteler expected his quirky friend to dress him down for drawing him without permission, but Jackson handed back the drawing, commenting that he had been very bad at drawing at West Point and admired those who had artistic ability. Jackson sat for only two photographs during the war. The Boteler drawing is one of the few illustrations of Jackson done from life and is proof of the often-quoted description of Jackson wearing his cap much lower than was the custom.

Continue up the road until it crests. Look to the right for the grave of Henry Kyd Douglas, the author of the book *I Rode with Stonewall*. Douglas was Jackson's youngest aide and therefore not the most trusted, but he was the best writer. His book is still popular today. His image has been taken down a notch or two in recent years, as historians have compared his book to the facts. Some have even speculated that it was Douglas who lost the copy of the secret orders describing Lee's Pennsylvania invasion plans, which resulted in the Battle of Sharpsburg.

Henry Kyd Douglas's grave in Shepherdstown

The view of Harpers Ferry from Maryland Heights

Harpers Ferry

Harpers Ferry is located off US 340 at the confluence of the Shenandoah and Potomac Rivers between Maryland and West Virginia. Today, the central core of the town is a national park that is open every day of the year. Jackson likely visited most, if not all, of the military buildings downtown, particularly the Armorer's House, which National Park Service research says served as his headquarters in early 1861. Jackson trained his troops on Bolivar Heights, located west of town on what is now National Park Service property. Call 304-535-6298 for information on the park. Jackson also spent some time at a private house at 1141 Washington Street that is now the Jackson Rose Bed & Breakfast.

Hardy hikers wishing to see for themselves what made Harpers Ferry a terrible town to try to defend can walk the path to the Maryland Heights overlook, located across the Potomac River and directly above the railroad tunnel. The hiking maps available from the National Park Service office give several options that run past both Confederate and Union sites. Be forewarned,

Harpers Ferry was Jackson's first real posting of the war. It also marked the first time he had been away from Anna, his wife, for any length of time. He kept in touch by writing soft, gentle letters that suggested a strong love—something that would have surprised his men and staff, who were used to a gruff, no-nonsense commander.

While staying at a private Harpers Ferry home in June 1861, Jackson wrote home, "I have a nice green yard, and if you were only here, how much we could enjoy it together! . . . My chamber is on the second story, and the roses climb even to that height, and come into my window, so that I have to push them out, when I want to lower it. I wish you could see with me the beautiful roses in the yard and garden, and upon the wall of the house here; but my sweet, little sunny face is what I want to see most of all."

Most casual students of the war assume that the first invasion of the North by Confederate forces came in September 1862, when

Jackson lived in this house, now the Jackson Rose Bed & Breakfast, for a time in Harpers Ferry.

Robert E. Lee's Army of Northern Virginia headed into Maryland on its way to Pennsylvania, only to be stopped at the Battle of Sharpsburg (or Antietam). But Colonel Thomas J. Jackson actually "invaded" the North in April 1861, not only without any orders from his commander, Robert E. Lee, but against Lee's express orders. Reacting to an obvious danger to his own forces at Harpers Ferry, Jackson placed several hundred men on Maryland Heights. Maryland was a slaveholding state that remained in the Union.

At first glance, Harpers Ferry would seem an important military asset, since it sat at the confluence of two rivers and had a railroad running right through town. In reality, the shallow, rocky bottoms made the rivers totally unsuited for riverboat travel. Commerce moved up and down the Potomac via the C & O Canal, which allowed the passage of small canal boats but could not accommodate military craft. The town was surrounded by mountains and ridges on three sides. Maryland Heights, the tallest ridge, towered more than 800 feet above Harpers Ferry. That meant that an enemy with cannons—even rifles—could easily rain fire on any occupying force and quickly control the town without much danger to itself.

Ordered to Harpers Ferry in April 1861 to defend that portion

The Armorer's House, Jackson's headquarters in Harpers Ferry

of western Virginia and to train the raw recruits who were flooding into the town in the days following the opening of the war, Jackson began to think of himself as an independent commander, rather than just the cog in the machine that he was supposed to be. Jackson, an artillerist during the Mexican War, immediately recognized the danger in defending the town and dispatched his men to Maryland Heights.

Counting all the recruits and the handful of cadets from Virginia Military Institute that Jackson had brought along to train the new citizen-soldiers, he had about 4,500 men. That was not nearly enough, in Jackson's mind. In one of the first letters he ever wrote to Robert E. Lee, Jackson asked for 5,500 more men and arms in the belief that the town would soon come under attack. As the full-scale war was barely a month old and the Confederate government was still organizing itself in Richmond, such a request was impossible to fulfill at best and ludicrous at worst. It was the first (but certainly not the last) time that Jackson demanded something impossible of his superiors or subordinates.

Lee replied in early May in his diplomatic (and sometimes frustratingly vague) way that the men and arms Jackson had requested would be sent as soon as possible. Lee then wrote, "It is considered advisable not to intrude upon the soil of Maryland unless compelled by the necessities of war. The aid of its citizens might be obtained in that quarter."

Jackson replied that he had already sent two companies onto Maryland Heights.

Lee wrote back, "I fear you have been premature in occupying the heights of Maryland with so strong a force near you. The true policy is to act on the defensive, and not invite an attack. If not too late you might withdraw until the proper time."

Jackson's prediction on the importance of Maryland Heights was proven true a year and a half later. In September 1862, several thousand men under Jackson arrived on Maryland Heights with a battery of cannons and rained shells down on the city and all the way to Bolivar Heights. Just as Jackson had warned, the Union soldiers holding the town had no way to respond to a bombardment from a great height. They were trapped and had to surrender.

In the months that Jackson was at Harpers Ferry in 1861, he did three things that helped create the legend that would continue to build for the next two years: he found a horse to suit him; he found a brigade to suit him; and he found a personal surgeon to suit him.

The horse was taken from a Union supply train captured as it was passing through the Harpers Ferry train station (today an Amtrak commuter stop). At first, Jackson picked a large mount that appeared to suit his five-foot-eleven frame. He also purchased a smaller horse from the same lot, planning to send it south to Lexington for his wife.

The larger horse soon proved to be unridable—at least by Jackson, who had developed a reputation for being a terrible horseman as far back as his days as a West Point cadet. He had an unbreakable habit of leaning far forward in the saddle, rather than sitting back as most horsemen do. Jackson's staff often described how the general's head appeared to be on a plane just above the head of the horse he was riding.

After rejecting the larger horse as unmanageable, Jackson got on the smaller horse. It did not exactly fit him like a glove; his big feet hung down well past where they should have. But something about the energy and gait of the "little sorrel" appealed to Jackson. Wife Anna never got her gift horse, but the general got a mount that would become almost as renowned as he over the next two years. Little Sorrel seemed to sense that he, too, was famous. Soldiers' diaries often mention how the horse seemed to throw up his head with pride whenever he galloped through a gauntlet of Jackson's cheering men. Years later, long after the war was over, Little Sorrel would prance and dance whenever he heard military music, a habit he had acquired while listening to military bands in the camps of the Army of Northern Virginia.

It was also at Harpers Ferry that Jackson acquired a brigade of his own. Those four (and later five) regiments were officially the First Virginia Brigade but came to be known after First Manassas as the Stonewall Brigade. The brigade was the only unit in the entire army to have a nickname officially recognized by the Confederate government.

The regiments that made up the brigade were the Second Virginia (from the area encompassing Winchester to Harpers Ferry), the Fourth Virginia (from the Rockbridge area), the Fifth Virginia (from the Staunton area), and the 27th Virginia (from the Lexington area). Later, the 33rd Virginia joined the unit.

At that point in the development of Confederate military organization, each brigade included an artillery battery. Jackson was assigned the four cannons of the Rockbridge Artillery, made up mostly of former V.M.I. cadets and led by a 52-year-old Episcopal pastor and friend of Lee, William Pendleton. The first guns in the unit were actually cannons that Jackson himself had commanded while instructing cadets at V.M.I. The six-pounders, about three-quarters the size of regular cannons, were designed so the cadets could move them around by hand. They soon proved to be impractical in field service and were returned to V.M.I., where they remain today.

The only flat spot near Harpers Ferry where the brigade could train was Bolivar Heights, a low ridge west of town where most of the recruits camped and where Jackson's V.M.I. cadets were turning them into soldiers. The training ground—which became a battleground in September 1862, when it was occupied by Union troops trying to resist Jackson—is part of the national park today. It includes walking trails with interpretive signs.

The last thing Jackson acquired at Harpers Ferry was the service of Dr. Hunter Holmes McGuire. McGuire, just 21 when assigned to the post of surgeon at Harpers Ferry, was almost rejected by the stern Jackson, who thought him too young. In time, McGuire won Jackson's confidence and became a key person on his staff. It was McGuire who later amputated Jackson's arm in the field hospital at Chancellorsville. He was also the attending doctor when Jackson breathed his last at Guinea Station.

After a few weeks at Harpers Ferry, Colonel Jackson was replaced by a general, Joseph Johnston, a West Point classmate of Lee's. Johnston quickly made up his own mind that the ridges surrounding the town made defending it untenable. He ordered the bridges leading into Harpers Ferry and all local military assets to be destroyed.

After making a movement on Harpers Ferry in May 1862 that preceded his Shenandoah Valley Campaign, Jackson returned to the town that September. He surrounded it on three sides and forced the surrender of more than 12,000 Union soldiers, the largest capture of American forces until World War II. Moving from School House Ridge west of Bolivar Heights through Bolivar and down into

Bolivar Heights in Harpers Ferry, where Jackson trained troops

the town, Jackson was surprised at the reaction he got. Hundreds of people were crowding to see him—and those were just the Union prisoners. Jackson was already a legend in the war. The Union soldiers wanted to get a good look at the man who could have rained death and destruction on them, but who instead paroled them after they surrendered. To the amusement of his men, and to Jackson's embarrassment, many of the Federals cheered and saluted him as he rode among them to get a close look at the town. One Federal was recorded to have said, "Had we been commanded by Jackson, we could not be where we are now."

Jackson did not stay in Harpers Ferry to savor his victory. Within a few hours of retaking the town, he and the bulk of his division were on their way to Sharpsburg to link up with the rest of Lee's army, which was digging in to await a Federal attack. It was the last time he saw the town where he first caught the attention of the Confederate army.

Charles Town

> Charles Town is a few miles southwest of Harpers Ferry on US 340.

Jackson was in Charles Town only a few times, but the first came at an important moment in American history. He bore witness to the coming of war when he was present at the hanging of abolitionist John Brown. The hanging took place at the corner of Hunter and Samuel Streets, four blocks south of the county courthouse on East Washington and George Streets. Samuel Street is one block east of George.

John Brown, a radical abolitionist who hacked a slaveholding family to death in Kansas in 1856, surfaced again in the country's consciousness when he led a raid on Harpers Ferry on October 16, 1859. Brown and his 18 followers walked into town over the Potomac River bridge with an audacious plan—they would capture the United States Armory at Harpers Ferry, then incite the slaves on the plantations around the town to begin a revolt that would spread from this corner of Virginia all the way through the South.

The plan fell apart the moment Brown walked into Harpers Ferry. Though he was successful in capturing the armory, angry townspeople reacted more like a militia than the frightened civilians he assumed they would be. They fought back, forcing him to retreat to a small building that stored the town's fire engine. The horde of slaves he imagined pouring into town never materialized. Instead, the few slaves who did join him were forced into the act as hostages. Within 24 hours of the raid's beginning, a force of United States Marines under the temporary command of United States Army lieutenant colonel Robert E. Lee captured Brown's raiders, killing 10 out of 19 but sparing Brown. He was tried, convicted, and sentenced to die by hanging in December.

The Harpers Ferry raid laid bare the differences between North

The site where John Brown was hanged in Charles Town

and South. The South looked on in horror as Northern newspapers praised Brown's raid and ignored his plan that slaves kill all the whites they could. The North looked upon the South with horror because it still kept slaves more than 30 years after the practice had been outlawed in the North.

As Brown's execution date drew near, rumors swept Virginia that the same wealthy men who had financed the raid on Harpers Ferry were now building an army to free him. On November 25, 1859, the governor of Virginia ordered a contingent of cadets from Virginia Military Institute to Charles Town to make sure the hanging was conducted as planned. The cadets were ordered to defend the state if any abolitionist army appeared. Jackson commanded the detachment.

He left nothing to chance on December 2, 1859, placing two cannons on either side of the gallows pointing outward, ready should an abolitionist army sneak into town and attack the gallows.

No such army appeared, and Brown's hanging was carried out in front of a crowd of spectators, militiamen, and army regulars, among them Lieutenant Colonel Lee. Jackson wrote a very detailed account of the hanging to his wife, even describing Brown's death-throe twitches. He also mentioned that he offered up a prayer for Brown.

The hanging and Jackson's response to it demonstrated how slavery had divided the nation. Brown was a religious fanatic who believed hacking people to death with axes was ordained by God. Jackson was a devout Presbyterian who thought Brown deserved to be executed for the murders he had committed, even if they were perpetrated in an attempt to end the institution of slavery.

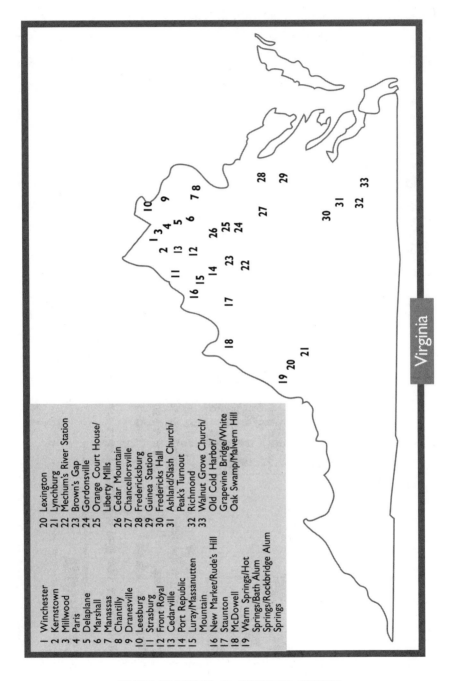

Virginia

1 Winchester
2 Kernstown
3 Millwood
4 Paris
5 Delaplane
6 Marshall
7 Manassas
8 Chantilly
9 Dranesville
10 Leesburg
11 Strasburg
12 Front Royal
13 Cedarville
14 Port Republic
15 Luray/Massanutten Mountain
16 New Market/Rude's Hill
17 Staunton
18 McDowell
19 Warm Springs/Hot Springs/Bath Alum Springs/Rockbridge Alum Springs
20 Lexington
21 Lynchburg
22 Mechum's River Station
23 Brown's Gap
24 Gordonsville
25 Orange Court House/ Liberty Mills
26 Cedar Mountain
27 Chancellorsville
28 Fredericksburg
29 Guinea Station
30 Fredericks Hall
31 Ashland/Slash Church/ Peak's Turnout
32 Richmond
33 Walnut Grove Church/ Old Cold Harbor/ Grapevine Bridge/White Oak Swamp/Malvern Hill

IN THE FOOTSTEPS OF STONEWALL JACKSON
54

Winchester

This town is located at the north end of the Shenandoah Valley where US 11 (once the Valley Turnpike) and I-81 intersect US 17/US 50. Winchester was the key to defending the vital valley early in the war and was Jackson's headquarters for several months during the winter of 1861-62. The Stonewall Jackson Headquarters Museum is at 415 North Braddock Street. Call 540-667-3242 for information.

Located just 30 miles southwest of Harpers Ferry (Jackson's first posting), about 40 miles directly south of the Potomac River, and 40 to 60 miles southeast of several Union-occupied towns in Maryland, Winchester was an obvious military target early in the war. Part of the reason was that the town lay at the north end of the Valley Turnpike, a 93-mile macadamized highway running from Winchester to Staunton. Made of crushed stone and a layer of tar to hold the rocks together, the turnpike was as fine a paved surface as could be found in the South. Troops, cavalry, and artillery could all use the turnpike to move swiftly up and down the Shenandoah Valley. Any force that controlled the road could move far more quickly than an enemy that

*The Taylor Hotel, Jackson's first
headquarters in Winchester*

had to use the standard dirt roads, which could turn to quagmires in rain and snow.

Colonel Jackson and his force arrived in the Winchester area in early June 1861 after leaving Harpers Ferry in the face of an advancing enemy. Jackson's men camped around Bunker Hill (now in West Virginia), located about 10 miles north of Winchester. After moving north to fight his first skirmish at Falling Waters, Jackson formally moved to Winchester in early July as a newly minted brigadier general, thanks to his handling of his troops at Falling Waters. He made his first headquarters at the Taylor Hotel, which still stands at 125 North Loudoun Street, though it is much changed architecturally. Loudoun Street is now a downtown shopping district that does not carry motor traffic.

It was from downtown Winchester on July 18, 1861, that Jackson and his as yet unfamous brigade began their secret march toward the Union forces that were moving on the railroad junction at Manassas, 60 miles away. As would be his practice during the war, Jackson did not tell his men where they were going or what they would do when they got there. Since the Federals were known to be as close as 25 miles to the north, most of the Confederates guessed they were going to attack them. Only after the march was well under way and heading east, not north, did Jackson stop and read the men an order from his commander, General Joseph Johnston, that told them they were "crossing the Blue Ridge" to help General Beauregard. No mention was made of Manassas.

Jackson noted that after hearing the purpose of their march, the men were filled with "eagerness and animation where before there had been only lagging and uninterested obedience." Here, on the first major march of the war, Jackson saw that the men got a surge of energy from knowing their purpose. But this was one of the few times Jackson gave his men any idea of where they were going, and he did it only under orders. In most future marches, even Jackson's generals didn't know where they were going. It is a mystery why he kept future destinations and purposes secret.

General Thomas Jackson returned to Winchester in November 1861 as Stonewall Jackson, the man who had saved the South at Manassas by standing firm in the face of a Federal attack. Jackson returned not as a mere brigadier but as general in command of "the Valley of Virginia," his assignment being to defend the Shenandoah Valley from all attacks. The man who had chafed under General Joseph Johnston's reluctance to allow him to attack at will now had an independent army that he could wield.

Not long after getting this command, Jackson proposed to use it to invade the North. He talked grandly about capturing and burning Philadelphia and Pittsburgh and moving all the way to Lake Erie to demonstrate to the North that it could be invaded as easily as it had invaded the South at Manassas. Jackson's bold plans fell on stunned ears. Southern politicians had no intention of invading the North. All they wanted at the moment was to set up a defense of the South while they waited for Europe to come in on their side. Jackson took the rejection of his ideas well enough. He was a good soldier. He would set about defending the Shenandoah Valley.

He again set up temporary headquarters in the Taylor Hotel that November. His first task was to assemble a force to defend his new command. He requested that his old brigade, now called the Stonewall Brigade after its famous former commander, be transferred to the valley. The Second, Fourth, Fifth, 27th, and 33rd Virginia Regiments comprised that brigade. Jackson also requested that other troops be assigned him, so he could create a real army instead of a department that existed only on paper.

It was here at the Taylor Hotel that Jackson's staff was startled to see his romantic side. In late December 1861, Anna, Jackson's wife, invited to come live with him at headquarters, arrived late at night on the stagecoach. Unsure what to do, as she had not had time to telegraph her husband that she would be arriving, Anna was about to step into the hotel lobby when a man came out of the shadows, grabbed her from behind, and started kissing her. It was Jackson, who had been riding down from his relocated headquarters each night checking the late stage arrivals in anticipation of seeing his wife.

While Jackson was consolidating his command in Winchester, he got both bad news and good news about blacks he had known in Lexington. From a letter his sister-in-law wrote him, he learned of the death of Amy, an elderly slave who had been his housekeeper and cook. Jackson wrote a return letter that the news of Amy's death had brought tears to his eyes. It was one of only two recorded times during the war that Jackson admitted to crying about the death of someone he knew. It was at about this same time that Jim Lewis, a middle-aged black man, probably a slave Jackson hired from another resident of Lexington, made his way to Winchester to become Jackson's personal servant. Jackson seems to have trusted Lewis implicitly, and Lewis seems to have enjoyed his employment, staying with Jackson until he breathed his last. Later, Lewis served Jackson aide Sandie Pendleton until Pendleton's own death on the battlefield. Lewis survived the war and returned to Lexington.

Jackson soon discovered that the nickname "Stonewall" attracted unwanted attention that kept him from fulfilling his duties. Within a few days of arriving in Winchester, he decided to move his headquarters about six blocks from the Taylor Hotel to a house at 415 North Braddock Street offered to him by Lieutenant Colonel Lewis T. Moore, the great-grand-father of actress Mary Tyler Moore. Jackson used the Moore House for only a few months. It was from there that he wrote a letter of resignation from the Confederate army.

Jackson visited the Taylor Hotel on at least one more occasion. He spent one night in the hotel after his men won the First Battle of Winchester—part of the famed Valley Campaign—on May 25, 1862.

At the Moore House—the site of the Stonewall Jackson Headquarters Museum today—Jackson formulated a winter campaign to capture Romney, a Union outpost about 50 miles west of Winchester. The bold plan offered an early look into the fighting style that became Jackson's trademark.

The Moore House, Jackson's second headquarters in Winchester, where he resigned from the Confederate army

Jackson intended to march as soon as he got a major force together. In late November, he requested that General William Loring's three brigades—then far away on Sewell Mountain in southwest Virginia—be ordered to Winchester to "cooperate" in Jackson's idea. The distinction was real. Loring had his own army and was not under direct obligation to Jackson, but he reluctantly agreed to come as long as his men would be properly clothed.

Winter campaigns had not enjoyed a good reputation in warfare since the severe Russian winter had stopped Napoleon from capturing Moscow in the early 1800s. History, however, had never hindered Jackson's thinking. He did not care about the threat of snow, ice, and cold weather. He just knew he wanted to capture Romney.

While waiting for Loring, Jackson led a foray from Winchester toward Dam Number Five on the Potomac River to keep his men in fighting trim. He and his troops had just returned from Dam Number Five when Anna arrived at the Taylor Hotel. Anna lived for several days at Jackson's headquarters at the Moore House, but it was obvious that the hustle and bustle of military responsibilities meant she would have to find somewhere else to sleep. The Reverend and Mrs. James Graham offered to put up the Jacksons at their home at 319 Braddock, just one block south of the headquarters; the home still stands today. The Jacksons eagerly accepted the offer, and it worked out for the best. The Jacksons felt comfortable with the Grahams. Their daughter was likely conceived in that home.

Loring's men arrived in Winchester around Christmas. Jackson gave them hardly any time to recover from the long march they had made to get there, leading them off toward Romney on January 1, 1862. It proved a disastrous campaign plagued by snow, ice, muddy roads, and men too exhausted to fight. The troops were pushed by an impatient general who could not understand why they were more interested in eating hot meals than sending hot lead into the enemy.

When Jackson returned from Romney three and a half weeks later, he considered the campaign a success, though few Federals had been killed or captured, few supplies had been secured, and Romney had been abandoned without a fight. What Jackson left at Romney were hundreds of sick and angry men and officers under Loring who felt they had been dragged over the Virginia mountains in the dead of winter, then been abandoned within easy striking distance of the Union.

On January 31, 1862, Jackson found a telegram from Secretary of War Judah P. Benjamin waiting for him at his headquarters at the Moore House. It instructed Jackson to order Loring back from Romney in anticipation of a Union attack.

Jackson promptly wrote Loring ordering him back to Winchester, then wrote a letter to Benjamin saying, "With such interference in my command I cannot expect to be of much service in the field; and accordingly respectfully request to be ordered to report for duty to the Superintendent of the Virginia Military Institute at Lexington, as has been done in the case of other professors. Should this application not be granted, I respectfully request that the President will accept my resignation from the Army."

When news of Jackson's resignation traveled around the army and Richmond, his friends sprang into action. Governor John Letcher stormed into Benjamin's office and demanded that the secretary apologize. Other friends begged Jackson to reconsider. Even President Davis, who had asked Benjamin to write the letter, had to backtrack in the face of officials who demanded to know what he would do if the most famous Confederate general in the army resigned. Within 10 days, Jackson was convinced to stay in the army, and the government officials resolved not to meddle in routine military affairs.

Jackson, always ready to hold a grudge, filed court-martial

charges against Loring, though it was actually Loring's subordinate officers who had reported Jackson to Richmond. Government officials wisely decided not to carry the incident any farther and refused to agree to Jackson's court-martial request. Loring was, however, stripped of his Virginia brigades, which were transferred to Jackson's command. Loring himself was transferred far out of Jackson's sight. Curiously, the Virginia regimental commanders who had signed the letter to Benjamin were left in place and were forced to deal with Jackson, who knew exactly who they were and what they had done.

In late February 1862, Jackson received one of his future keys to success when Lieutenant Keith Boswell walked into the Moore House to join his staff as an engineering officer. The 21-year-old would team within a month with 33-year-old lieutenant Jed Hotchkiss to find the roads and draw the maps that would make Stonewall Jackson the master of the Shenandoah Valley.

In the first weeks of March, the Federal army began organizing a move south toward Winchester. For safety reasons, Anna had to leave. She had spent nearly three months with her husband at his headquarters and in the Presbyterian manse. It would be 13 months before she would see him again in Fredericksburg. By then, she would be able to show Jackson the daughter born while her father was in the field.

On March 11, Jackson held a meeting of his regimental colonels. He told them he intended to launch a night attack on the Federals, who were moving on Winchester from the north. He ordered that the supply wagons were to be moved just south of town and that the men were to follow them, which would give the Federals the impression that Jackson was abandoning the town and retreating. Instead, Jackson intended for the men to eat their rations just outside town, then move quietly back into Winchester and head north to hit the Federals in a surprise attack. Jackson's officers were reluc-

*The Presbyterian manse in Winchester
where Jackson and his wife Anna lived*

tant to go along with a rare night attack.

The plan became moot when Jackson learned that the supply wagons had gone an extra eight miles and that the troops had followed them. Launching the attack would require the men to march all night just to get into place. Jackson reluctantly abandoned his plan to save Winchester from capture and rode out of town.

On a slight ridge south of town, Jackson and his surgeon, Dr. Hunter Holmes McGuire, looked back at Winchester. Jackson, still angry with his officers for not agreeing with his plan, said, "That is the last council of war I will ever hold." He kept his word. In every subsequent attack, few of his officers knew what he was planning to do until they got his express orders just before they were to execute them.

Jackson returned briefly to the town on May 25, 1862, to fight the First Battle of Winchester, the fourth battle of his Valley Campaign. All of the Winchester battlefield has disappeared under commercial and residential construction over the years. The area that was Jackson's main objective is now a high school and a neighborhood about a half-mile southwest of the historic downtown. Jackson spent the night in the Taylor Hotel while in town.

After making a quick run up to harass the Federals at Harpers Ferry, he went through Winchester again. He finally departed on May 31, heading toward Port Republic.

Jackson passed though Winchester again in October and November 1862, prior to the move toward Fredericksburg. For a few days in November, he made his headquarters in a house on the southwest corner of Washington Street and Fairfax Lane. This home was almost within sight of the Graham House, where he had enjoyed a few months with Anna.

It was on one of these short trips to Winchester that a legendary story about Jackson was born. On November 1, 1862, he had lunch at the home of Dr. McGuire, located at the northeast corner of North Braddock and Amherst Streets. During the meal, McGuire's sister told the general that she had a favor to ask of him. He heartily agreed without knowing what it would be.

"I want you to have your photograph taken for me," she said.

Jackson had not sat for a photograph in several years. After one

The home on Washington Street that was Jackson's third headquarters in Winchester

and a half years of armed conflict, there was no wartime photograph of Stonewall Jackson.

To everyone's surprise, Jackson agreed. He got up immediately from the table and headed for the photography studio of Nathaniel Routzahn, which was on the west side of Loudoun Street just south of its intersection with what is now Boscawen Street. The Reverend Graham accompanied Jackson. When Jackson sat for the photograph, the reverend noticed that the general was missing a button on his jacket. Jackson immediately took off the coat and sewed on the button. The amused Graham noted that Jackson could find the Union forces and smash them at will, but he could not sew a button in line with the others. The full-face photograph of Jackson—the only one taken during the war—shows one button distinctly out of line with the others. Anna Jackson later said the photograph was her favorite image of her husband. The usually dour Jackson seems to have a slight smile on his face.

These short stays were crowded with intensive military planning. Never again did Winchester see a happy, contented Stonewall Jackson. Actually, once Jackson rode out of town in November 1862, it never saw him again at all.

Kernstown

This small community lies a couple of miles southwest of Winchester. The recently preserved battlefield where the Battle of Kernstown was fought is on US 11 near its intersection with VA 706 just north of Ocquon Presbyterian Church. At the time of this writing, the battlefield could be viewed only from a distance. An interpretive marker is in the church parking lot. Visible in the distance is a stone wall from which the Confederates fought.

The Kernstown battlefield

It is one of the odd things about the legend of Stonewall Jackson that the only battle he truly lost from a tactical standpoint turned out to be a strategic victory. On top of that, he lost the first battle in a campaign that would solidify the Jackson mystique.

In mid-March 1862, Union general George McClellan began his march on Richmond up the peninsula between the York and James Rivers. He intended to mass all possible troops in order to overwhelm the Confederates.

Understandably, President Lincoln was worried that Jackson's 4,600 troops in the Shenandoah Valley (later to be joined by 12,000 more) would seize the opportunity when Union troops were pulled all the way down to Richmond. Lincoln had heard of Jackson's aggressiveness at First Manassas. He demanded that McClellan leave some troops to keep Jackson at bay.

Union general Nathaniel Banks was ordered to keep his corps of 38,000 troops near Manassas to protect Washington. One of Banks's divisions under General James Shields was then near Winchester and ready to pull back. Jackson sent Colonel Turner Ashby's cavalry to harass Shields. Ashby fought a skirmish in Winchester with a handful of Shields's men on March 22. Based on that little fight, and after literally asking the people of Winchester where the Yankees were,

Ashby reported back to Jackson that the town was held by only a few regiments of Federals, who were preparing to flee to Harpers Ferry. Ashby never rode north of Winchester. Had he done so, he would have seen a full division of Federals who were in no hurry to go anywhere.

The next day, Jackson moved his little force toward Winchester, which he had left just a few weeks earlier. As he neared Kernstown, he saw some Federals on a hill. He pushed his men toward them, thinking they represented the bulk of the opposing force. Within minutes, Federals came rushing down on Kernstown from Winchester.

Jackson looked at the onrushing troops and quietly told his chief aide, "We are in for it."

They were. While Jackson had assumed he would be attacking a force about half the size of his own, he actually faced a force several times the size of his. At one point in the battle, the Stonewall Brigade, under the command of General Richard Garnett, found itself out of ammunition, so it retreated. A furious Jackson demanded that it return to the line. Garnett pleaded that his men had run out of ammunition. Jackson replied that they still had bayonets. Jackson later filed court-martial charges against Garnett for having his men retreat without orders. Only darkness saved Jackson's entire command from being overrun. That day, Jackson lost one-fourth of his force. During the night, he moved the survivors south up the Valley Turnpike (today's US 11).

Jackson forgave Ashby for the mistake that decimated his infantry. In fact, he put Ashby's name up for general within a few weeks.

Jackson clearly lost the Battle of Kernstown, but that made no difference to Lincoln. Frightened that Jackson had merely withdrawn temporarily, and convinced that Jackson's force was much larger than it actually was (thanks to inflated numbers supplied by the victorious Shields), Lincoln pulled troops from around Washington and sent them to the Shenandoah Valley. The troops McClellan wanted to help him attack Richmond would not be coming—all because Stonewall's 4,600 men were defeated at Kernstown.

Millwood

The tiny community of Millwood lies 11 miles east of Winchester, just north of the intersection of US 17 and VA 255. Located here is Carter Hall, now the headquarters for Project Hope, an international aid organization.

One of the first stops Jackson and his men made on July 18, 1861, on the way to First Manassas was on the land around Carter Hall, a large brick house built by a Revolutionary War colonel. As the men filled their canteens from nearby springs and wells, ladies from the surrounding area came with food. War was still a festive thought in those early days, and the men were about to vanquish the enemy in one large battle.

Jackson returned to Carter Hall in November 1862. The owners offered to let him use the house as a headquarters, but Jackson refused, saying he did not want men muddying up its floors. Instead, he pitched a tent in the front yard. It was at Carter Hall that Jackson got confirmation that his promotion to lieutenant general had been approved. Jackson, who had never risen above regular lieutenant or brevet major in the United States Army, was now one of the highest-ranking officers in the Confederate army.

This was a critical time for the Army of Northern Virginia. Jackson had about 38,000 men—the entire Second Corps—camped in the fields around Millwood. Longstreet and the First Corps were around Front Royal. Everyone was waiting to see what the Army of the Potomac under newly appointed Union general Ambrose Burnside would do.

The cold, damp weather aggravated Jackson's health, but he refused to move into Carter Hall. Instead, he went back to Winchester for a few days to an empty house on Washington Street near his headquarters of the previous year. He stayed there only a few days before getting frantic orders from Lee that Burnside had suddenly started moving on Fredericksburg. Once he left the valley on November 25, 1862, Jackson never returned.

Two miles southeast of Carter Hall on US 17 is a bridge over the Shenandoah River near what was known as Berry's Ford during the war. When Jackson's men reached this point on the way to First Manassas in July 1861, it was the first time they forded a major river. It was certainly not the last. The men dried from their waist-deep trip across the Shenandoah, and the air cooled as night fell. Still, Jackson pushed his men forward, the goal being to get over Ashby's Gap, which would mark their departure from the valley.

Carter Hall in Millwood, where Jackson was promoted to lieutenant general

Paris, Virginia, the village that gave birth to the
legend of Stonewall standing lone guard over his men

Paris

*This village lies about seven miles southeast of Millwood. It is
just off US 17 less than a half-mile beyond Ashby's Gap. It
looks much as it did in 1861.*

About two o'clock in the morning on July 19, 1861, the head of
Jackson's army reached Paris, which is still an idyllic little village
today. Here, Jackson finally called a halt to the march toward First
Manassas. The men dropped and fell instantly asleep.

General Bernard Bee's cry at First Manassas—"There stands Jackson like a stone wall!"—is generally considered the first Jackson legend. The incident that occurred at Paris actually preceded it, though
it likely did not become part of the Jackson legend until after his
death.

In a letter to Anna after the stop in Paris, Jackson wrote off-
handedly, "My men were so exhausted that I let them sleep while I
kept watch myself."

Somehow, that simple sentence got into the public domain. Perhaps Anna mentioned it to friends and they told and retold it. By the time Jackson's biographers heard about it years later, the sentence had grown into a story that Jackson himself was a single guard keeping watch over a sleeping brigade numbering 2,600 men. One soldier even wrote a poem about how he watched his general—"a lonesome sentinel"—riding around the camp all night.

Writing after the war, Jackson's brother-in-law, D. H. Hill, called the whole story "monstrously absurd" and said it "reflects but little credit on Jackson as a soldier."

If the story were true, Lee would have relieved Jackson of command, as the incident would have demonstrated Jackson to be an incredibly careless, derelict general who would risk the safety of his entire command when he had no real idea from what direction the enemy might attack. Jackson might have embellished his role as a guard in order to tease or impress his wife, but there is little doubt that he had every regiment post pickets. Likely, there were dozens of sleepy—but awake—guards on duty that night. If the stern, by-the-book Jackson had caught those pickets sleeping, he would have had them arrested and probably shot.

What really happened, according to Jackson's surgeon, Dr. Hunter Holmes McGuire, was that Jackson, who had been at the head of his men, intended to stay awake until the end of the column filed into the village. Instead, McGuire convinced Jackson to go ahead and get some sleep, while he, McGuire, made sure the tail-end artillery stopped in the village. Jackson slept.

Piedmont Station (present-day Delaplane), where Jackson's men loaded on trains for First Manassas

Delaplane

Delaplane, known as Piedmont Station during the war, is located along US 17 at the railroad crossing about seven miles south of Paris.

After a few hours of sleep in the village of Paris in the early morning on July 19, 1861, Jackson rousted his men and resumed the march toward First Manassas. He had them at Piedmont Station before eight o'clock that morning. Delaplane looks much like it probably did in those days. A couple of buildings lie beside the railroad tracks, and some houses are nearby.

What happened next had never before occurred in warfare. Jackson loaded his men on railroad cars on the Manassas Gap Railroad. From Piedmont Station, they would make the 34 miles to Manassas Gap Junction by rail. It was a jolting, eight-hour trip, but one that would have taken two exhausting days if the men had continued marching. The actual transfer of General Joseph Johnston's entire infantry ranks by rail would take two full days.

Using the railroad to get to the fighting front was likely Johnston's idea, but by being the initial general to ride the train to Manassas, Jackson scored another first in the war. He had already been among the first to train soldiers to face the enemy when he took V.M.I. cadets to Richmond in April. He had been the first to set up defenses against the Union at Harpers Ferry. He had been the first to actually invade Northern territory when he fortified Maryland Heights above Harpers Ferry. And he had been among the first to cross swords with the Union when he fought the skirmish at Falling Waters on July 2, 1861.

Marshall

This town lies several miles southeast of Delaplane off VA 55 / I-66. It retains little of its 1862 appearance.

Jackson visited Marshall, called Salem during the war, in August 1862 on the way to Second Manassas. Jackson's men had stolen a flank march on Union general John Pope from just north of Culpeper (located south of here) through villages like Amisville and Orlean, then into Salem from what is now CR 647.

As the sun was setting on August 25, Jackson pulled to the side of the road south of Salem and climbed on a large rock to watch the column of men marching past him. The weary men started to cheer, but Jackson simply raised his hand to quiet them. They were deep behind Union lines, and he did not want any sound to give them away. When the men obeyed his unspoken order, Jackson turned to an aide and gave his highest compliment: "Who could not conquer with troops such as these?"

Just east of Marshall on I-66 is Thoroughfare Gap, a mountain pass through which the Confederates passed on their way to Second Manassas. Farther east off I-66 are the small towns of Haymarket and Gainesville, which were surprised to see Jackson's troops in August 1862. Bristoe Station lies just east of the intersection of VA 28 and CR 619. Jackson sent his men up the roadbed of the Orange & Alexandria Railroad toward Manassas Junction, rather than boldly marching them down the Warrenton Turnpike.

Manassas

Manassas is quickly becoming a suburb of Washington, D.C., which is threatening its Civil War history. The town lies about 40 miles southwest of the nation's capital at the junction of VA 28 and VA 234. It was from Washington that the Union troops of General Irvin McDowell started their quest to defeat the Confederates of General P. G. T. Beauregard on July 20, 1861.

Manassas National Battlefield is just north of the VA 234 North exit off I-66. It is about a half-mile to the park entrance and another half-mile to the intersection with US 29. Jackson played prominent roles at both First Manassas on July 21, 1861, and Second Manassas on August 29 and 30, 1862. The key Jackson sites at First Manassas are around his bronze statue on Henry House Hill, around the two Union cannon positions that could have wrecked his line, and around Young's Branch, where his broken finger was dressed. The key Jackson site for Second Manassas is the Unfinished Railroad Cut. You can reach the cut by turning south or left on US 29 and proceeding to CR 622 (Featherbed Lane). Turn right and drive until you see the Unfinished Railroad Cut parking lot. Call 703-361-1339 for information. A small fee is charged to visit the park.

The Manassas Museum is downtown at 9171 Prince William Street. It lies across the street from what was Manassas Junction during the war. Jackson's men captured large quantities of Union army goods there in August 1862. The museum puts most of its focus on the postwar rebuilding of the city. Call 703-368-1873 for details.

The politicians of both North and South figured the same thing in the early spring and summer of 1861: one large battle would settle the war. The Union believed that after one big fight, the Southerners would run and the Union army would march down to Richmond, arrest Jefferson Davis and the Confederate Congress, and start the process of re-forming the Union. The South believed that after one big fight, the Union army would lose its taste for combat and that President Abraham Lincoln would let the South go about its business of leaving the Union.

Lincoln in particular was a big believer in getting one big battle under way. When General Irvin McDowell protested that his army of new recruits was little more than an armed mob of untrained clerks, Lincoln replied, "You are green. They are green. You are all green together." Lincoln made no bones about it. Either McDowell would put his army in the field immediately to fight the Confederates or he would find some general who would.

The Confederates correctly figured that Manassas Junction, a railroad head just 40 miles from Washington, would be a key Union target. If the Federals could capture Manassas Junction, they could get a toehold in the South for sending supplies to distant armies.

General P. G. T. Beauregard would set up his defenses there and wait for the Federals to come to him.

Jackson's men, under the overall command of General Joseph Johnston, arrived by train at Manassas Junction—located across the street from what is now the Manassas Museum—the day before the battle. A surprised Beauregard gave Johnston's troops a place in line. Actually, Beauregard was sorry to see Johnston's men arriving by train. He had hoped they would march in from the west, which would have put them on McDowell's exposed flank.

On July 21, Jackson moved into position on the southeast slope of a slight hill called Henry House Hill, after the family that lived in the house there. About a mile north of Jackson's position was Sudley Springs, where the Federals were crossing Bull Run in massed numbers, pushing hard against a much smaller force of Southerners that included General Bernard Bee. Jackson ordered his men to lie prone on the reverse slope of the hill, which was covered with tall grass, while he rode forward to the crest to survey the situation.

It did not look good. Swarms of Federals were sweeping across Bull Run, the little creek in the distance, and heading Jackson's way. The outnumbered Confederate troops in front of Jackson's Virginians could not form and hold a line. Artillery shells began to crash into the reverse slope of the hill, killing and wounding a number of Jackson's men. Still, he ordered them to lie in the grass and not show themselves.

At one point in the battle—actually, before any of his men fired—Jackson threw his left arm into the air, either in prayer or in his habit of raising his arms in the belief that it helped drain blood back into his body. He soon jerked the arm back down. His middle finger had been nicked by a bullet.

As the enemy crossed the turnpike (now US 29) in front of him, Jackson saw a general riding toward him. It was Bernard Bee of South

Carolina. The two knew each other but may not have met face to face in years. Bee told Jackson, "General, they are driving us."

Jackson looked toward the Federals and replied calmly, "Sir, we will give them the bayonet."

It was a brave, stern statement, but not one Jackson's men wanted to hear. By the Civil War, rifling had increased the effective range of a musket from 100 yards to 400 yards. The bayonet—the prime weapon of colonial troops once their smooth-bore flintlocks had been fired—was now useless, since a trained rifleman could load and fire a rifled musket three times in a minute.

Bee looked at Jackson, then rode down to his men, who were swarming back toward Jackson's position. Bee pointed up the hill and said something very close to this: "Look, men, there is Jackson standing like a stone wall. Let us determine to die here and we will conquer. Rally round the Virginians."

Virginia historians have always maintained that Bee was praising Jackson for holding his line in the face of an advancing enemy. South Carolina historians have wondered if Bee was criticizing Jackson for not moving his men to come to Bee's aid. Some have even questioned if Bee said it at all.

By now, Jackson's men were standing and fighting, holding their ground just like a stone wall. On their left, two Federal artillery batteries of 11 rifled guns under Captains James Ricketts and Charles Griffin moved into position to rake Jackson's line. Some of J. E. B. Stuart's Confederate cavalry swept the Federal artillery's supporting infantrymen away, leaving the guns exposed. Jackson's 33rd Virginia, without orders from Jackson, started moving toward the Federal guns. Griffin had moved three guns even closer to Jackson's line and was ready to fire on the advancing 33rd Virginia, whose men were dressed in the blue they had always worn. But Griffin's commander, Colonel William Barry, rode up and ordered him not to fire on the advancing troops.

The Ricketts's battery, set up to fire down Jackson's line at First Manassas

Barry insisted that since the men were dressed in blue, they must be Federal reenforcements. Griffin protested that the troops were coming from the Confederate side, so they must be Southerners dressed in blue. Barry refused to change his order. Griffin's men, knowing they were right, watched helplessly as Jackson's 33rd Virginia poured a murderous volley into them.

The 33rd captured the guns, but more Federal infantry came up and decimated the regiment. The entire left side of the Confederate line began to falter. Then Jackson turned to his two fresh regiments, the Fourth and the 27th Virginia, which had been waiting behind his guns. Following a furious blast of cannon fire, the Virginians rushed forward. Jackson ordered them to "yell like furies." This was presumably the first time in the war that the Rebel yell was heard.

The Confederates slowly pushed the Federals off Henry House Hill. At one point, Jackson rounded up a number of stragglers, organized them, and told them that if they saw any Federals, they were to "give them pepper." "And salt too!" he added as an afterthought. This was about the best Jackson ever did at cursing.

While Jackson's brigade spearheaded the winning counterattack, it was the arrival of two fresh Confederate brigades from the train depot that finally won the battle after five o'clock that afternoon.

The cannons located at this position would have raked Jackson's line if his men had not captured them.

The battle over, Jackson decided to get treatment for his still-bleeding finger. The first doctor he saw casually said he would amputate it. Jackson rode off to find his own physician, Dr. Hunter Holmes McGuire, who had set up an aid station at the northeast side of Henry House Hill next to Young's Branch, a part of the battlefield that had just been vacated by the Federals. McGuire looked at the finger and said it was broken but that it could be saved. He put a splint on the finger and suggested that Jackson soak it in cold water. McGuire may not have known about Jackson's fascination with water cures. Regardless, his treatment was a much better alternative than cutting off Jackson's finger.

At that point, President Jefferson Davis rode to the field hospital where Jackson was being treated. It may have been the first time they met. Some historians believe that Jackson challenged Davis right there to follow the Federals all the way to Washington, where the Confederates could capture Abe Lincoln himself. Other historians dispute that any conversation took place between the two men.

The Confederates did not follow the Federals, since they were hardly in better shape than the men they had just defeated. In fact, the Confederates had lost more men than the Federals and were just as disorganized. Had Beauregard been able to reorganize his army at all, it would have taken several days. By that time, the Federal forces in Washington would have been organized behind breastworks.

The statue of Jackson outside the visitor center at Manassas National Battlefield makes him look like a bodybuilder with huge biceps, an artistic style used in the 1930s, when the statue was placed. While Jackson actually did work out with weights, he was not overly muscular. The statute stands on the spot where Jackson rode to look down into the valley and across to Matthews Hill to watch the progress of the Federals. His troops, lying prone in the tall grass behind him, were not visible to the Federals climbing the slight slope of Henry Hill. Cannons behind and in front of the visitor center mark the two Union battery positions that had the best chance of

Jackson statue where he faced the Federals at First Manassas

The view toward Matthews Hill, from which the Federals came at First Manassas

stopping Jackson's brigade. Once they were silenced and captured, the way was open for the Confederates to counterattack and sweep the Federals from the field.

The aid station where Jackson rode to be treated for his broken finger was located down Henry House Hill next to Young's Branch, about 30 yards from where US 29 runs today. This was also the spot where Jackson met President Jefferson Davis.

Second Manassas took place on August 29 and 30, 1862. It came about as a result of a campaign by General Robert E. Lee to figure out some way to get at Union general John Pope, who was facing Lee near Culpeper. Pope had brought a new concept of war to Virginia—attacking civilians and destroying their property without engaging the Confederate army. The attacks on civilians enraged Lee, who labeled Pope a "miscreant."

To get Pope to move out of his defenses, Lee sent Jackson on a march around Pope's right flank. Jackson moved quickly to Bristoe Station, then to Manassas Junction, where he captured tons of foodstuffs maintained by the Federals. Pope turned his back to Lee's half of the army and began marching to his rear to find Jackson, which was exactly what Lee wanted him to do. Now, Pope was in the open

The site where Jackson's broken finger was set along Young's Branch at First Manassas

between the two halves of the Confederate army.

Jackson's men occupied a woods beside and overlooking the Warrenton Turnpike (today's US 29). On the evening of August 28, a division of 10,000 Federals was marching east on the turnpike when Jackson opened up on its flank from the woods to the northwest. The Battle of Groveton, sometimes counted as part of Second Manassas, thus opened.

Groveton ended in a draw with heavy casualties on both sides, but now Jackson was in a jam. Pope knew where he was, and Pope was ahead of Longstreet's part of the Confederate army. If Pope could get the whole of his army to Manassas before Longstreet brought up his troops, Jackson could be caught in a Union army pincer.

Jackson moved his lines into an unfinished railroad cut about a mile northwest of where he had hit the Federals on the turnpike at Groveton. The railroad cut formed a natural trench line that made an excellent defense against Pope.

On August 29, the Federals hit Jackson's line again and again. They failed to penetrate but caused casualties all the same. Longstreet's men arrived to reenforce the Confederate line, something that the Federals never noticed. That night, Jackson shortened his line, which meant moving some of his men deeper into the woods. From the Federals' perspective, it looked like some portions of the Confederate line had been abandoned. Word began to filter back to Pope's headquarters that the Confederates had retreated.

By Sunday, August 30, Pope convinced himself that Jackson had retreated. More importantly, he also convinced himself that Longstreet was not on the field, though Longstreet's corps had actually moved into the trenches the previous night.

Pope ordered an attack on what he assumed would be Jackson's single corps moving in retreat in the open. What he found was two corps in trenches waiting to receive him. The Union attack started on the Confederate left. Jackson's men ran so short of ammunition that they resorted to throwing rocks at the Federals. The Federals, also short of ammunition, began throwing rocks back. On at least one part of the line, Second Manassas became a rock fight.

*The Unfinished Railroad Cut, into which
Jackson's men were sent at Second Manassas*

Longstreet waited until the Federals committed themselves, then ordered his artillery to open on the Union left. The Federals, who had no idea Longstreet was on the field, were shocked by the heavy artillery fire coming right into their faces. The whole left half of the Federal line collapsed and began to flee in the direction of Henry House Hill. Longstreet then unleashed his 25,000-man corps to chase them down. When Longstreet charged, the Federal right, too, began to retreat. The pressure on Jackson—who had stood alone against the entire Union army for nearly two days—was off.

Jackson was riding through his lines when he came upon some wounded Federals. He looked down and recognized a mortally wounded major. The officer was the son of Dr. Lowry Barney, who had treated Jackson with a water cure in upstate New York more than 10 years earlier. Jackson took time to write a note of regret to his old doctor, telling him that the Confederates would take care of the body of his son until he came to claim it.

Longstreet and Jackson chased the Federals to Henry House Hill, the same battlefield where the nickname "Stonewall" had been coined. There, the Federals created their own version of a stone wall. They dug in and refused to be pushed off the hill. The stubborn rear-line defense stopped the Confederates in their tracks while the rest of

*The Unfinished Railroad Cut at Second Manassas,
where Jackson's men withstood the Federal attack*

the Union army retreated toward Washington. Had the forces of Jackson and Longstreet been larger, and had the two generals been able to organize their men quickly enough, the Confederates might have overwhelmed the rear guard and made an attack on the retreating army.

Lee would never again come as close to totally destroying an army in open combat as he did on August 30, 1862. But he would try one more time. That was on September 1, 1862, two days later, when Jackson attempted to rush ahead of Pope's army in a bloody rear-guard action that would be called the Battle of Chantilly.

Jackson's headquarters at Second Manassas was in a tent beside the Rockbridge Artillery in the Unfinished Railroad Cut. Visitors can follow the National Park Service map to walk the entire cut. Jackson rode all up and down this line encouraging his men to throw back the Federals.

Chantilly

No battlefield has been lost to development to a greater degree than Chantilly, also known as Ox Hill. Surrounding a four-and-a-half-acre city park that has monuments to two Union generals who lost their lives at this savage battle are shopping centers, apartment complexes, and parking lots. Chantilly is just west of Fairfax Court House. Take the West Ox Road (CR 608) exit off US 50 north of I-66. Drive west for half a mile on West Ox Road, then turn right on Monument Drive. The wooded park on the left at this intersection is all that is left to recall the battle that raged all across the area.

Lee not only wanted to beat General John Pope's army at Second Manassas, he wanted to crush it. On August 31, 1862, the day after Pope had made a slow but orderly retreat from the battlefield, Lee ordered Jackson to try to get in front of Pope, who was heading back to Washington. If Jackson could stop Pope, Longstreet could come in from Pope's rear, and again the Confederates could work a pincer movement against the Federals.

Though his men had hardly rested or drawn rations after winning Second Manassas, and though rain was falling, Jackson took off after Pope. He tried a parallel road, hoping that a fast, secret march would put him in front. That was not to be. Pope marched just as fast in retreat as Jackson did in attack. Pope's rear guard saw Jackson coming, so surprise was out of the question.

Jackson halted his march near a home called Chantilly with the intent of waiting for Longstreet. The Federals, sensing that they had just a part of the Confederate army in front of them, attacked. The prey thus became the hunter.

The battle was fought in a downpour so heavy that the men could not always see what was in front of them. Lightning strikes killed some troops. The ammunition of both sides became so wet that much of it was useless.

Two Union generals died in the battle. One of them was one-armed Mexican War veteran Phil Kearny, who accidentally rode into Jackson's line because of confusion in the heavy rain.

The battle ended as a draw, both sides losing about 500 men. Pope continued his retreat to Washington. Jackson did not follow.

Within a few days, Jackson's force started marching northwest toward Leesburg. What the men did not know until they crossed the Potomac several miles northeast of Leesburg was that they were invading the North for the first time. It was something Jackson had been asking the South to do since April 1861.

The site of Jackson's Chantilly headquarters is now the parking lot of an apartment complex.

Dranesville

Dranesville is on VA 7 northwest of Washington, D.C. There is little here from Jackson's day.

It was near Dranesville that the long-simmering feud between Jackson and A. P. Hill boiled over on September 4, 1862.

The previous night, Jackson had given his division commanders marching orders for the next morning. But at the appointed hour for the march, Jackson discovered that half of Hill's men were still eating breakfast and filling their canteens. Worse, Jackson soon witnessed that Hill was not allowing his men the required 10-minute rest period after 50 minutes of walking. Jackson ordered Hill's column to stop, a breach of military etiquette, since he was not in direct command of the division. When Hill learned of this action, he rode up to Jackson, pulled his sword from his belt, and fairly shouted, "I submit my resignation, sir!" While it may sound silly for a general to resign because his men had been ordered to stop marching by a superior general, it was a matter of honor in those days that no general supersede the responsibilities of another. Jackson did not take the sword but told Hill he was under arrest.

Robert E. Lee later mediated—but failed to resolve—the dispute between the two generals at the Boyd House in Bunker Hill. Relations between Hill and Jackson remained frigid until Jackson's death.

*Big Spring north of Leesburg, where Jackson's men
filled their canteens before invading Maryland*

Leesburg

Leesburg, named after the Lee family, is located at the intersection of VA 7 and US 50 just south of the Potomac River about 12 miles west of Dranesville and about 50 miles northwest of Washington. The house where Jackson met with Lee before invading Maryland is a private business today.

A few hours after the confrontation between Jackson and A. P. Hill near neighboring Dranesville, the Confederate column arrived in Leesburg. Jackson marched the men to Big Spring, located on what is now US 15 North about 2.4 miles north of downtown beside the intersection with Tutt Road. The spring still flows. Gone is the George W. Ball House, where Jackson made his headquarters. It was at the George W. Ball House that Jackson questioned a Maryland-born colonel, Bradley Johnson, about the attitudes of the people they would encounter. Colonel Johnson warned Jackson that while Maryland was a slave state, it was filled with Unionists.

Jackson and Colonel Johnson rode to the home of Henry Harrison at 205 North King Street in downtown Leesburg, Lee's temporary

The Henry Harrison House in Leesburg, where Jackson and Lee discussed invading Maryland

headquarters. A human-relations consulting business stands there today. Johnson repeated what he had told Jackson. Lee and Johnson then turned to ask Jackson's opinion. He was fast asleep, sitting bolt upright.

The next afternoon, September 5, 1862, the Army of Northern Virginia began to wade across the Potomac River into Maryland. The first Southern invasion of the North was under way.

Strasburg

This town is about 15 miles northwest of Front Royal on US 11, which closely parallels I-81. The Stonewall Jackson Museum, located at 33229 Old Valley Pike one mile south of Exit 298 off I-81, has maps explaining Jackson's Valley Campaign. Call 540-465-5884 for information.

Jackson passed through Strasburg on numerous occasions but never did battle here.

The railroad running through town was the scene of heavy activity in April 1861, when Jackson's men reassembled the locomotives that had been dismantled at Martinsburg and pulled down the Valley Turnpike (today's US 11) by horse teams. This is still considered one of the most unusual feats of military equipment recovery in American history.

Prospect Hill Cemetery in Front Royal. Jackson attacked the Federal garrison from there.

Front Royal

Located at the intersection of US 340 / US 522 and I-66, Front Royal was the site of the third battle of Jackson's Valley Campaign. The battle was fought on May 23, 1862.

The Warren Rifles Museum is at 95 Chester Street; the Belle Boyd Cottage is behind it. The museum has some artifacts from the battle. Call 540-636-6982 for information.

If one does not count the Battle of McDowell (which was actually fought in the Allegheny Mountains) and Jackson's loss at Kernstown, the Battle of Front Royal may be considered the start of his famed Valley Campaign.

When Jackson's forces showed up on the heights of Prospect Hill Cemetery, just off Royal Avenue (US 340), it was as if they had risen out of the graves. The Federals occupying the town had no idea where Jackson was, but it was not supposed to be in the town cemetery, raining artillery shells down on them.

Jackson had marched from McDowell, west of Staunton, over two mountain ranges into Luray, then turned north roughly along what is now US 340. His men passed still-standing Asbury Methodist Church on US 340 and swept in on the unsuspecting, undermanned Federal garrison holding Front Royal.

Some say that 18-year-old Belle Boyd helped convince Jackson that the town could easily be taken. She ran from the town across open fields to deliver a message to Jackson that the local garrison was weak. Jackson likely already knew that and did not truly benefit from the teenager's message, but a legend was born that Boyd helped Jackson win the Battle of Front Royal.

There really wasn't much of a battle, at least in Front Royal. After shelling the Federals from the cemetery, Jackson's men, led by the First Maryland Regiment—Confederates who were anxious to do battle with the First Maryland Regiment of Federal troops—

The Belle Boyd Cottage in Front Royal

pushed into town. The Federals fled over the two bridges that spanned the two forks of the Shenandoah River, which runs just north of town.

The Shenandoah River in Front Royal, over which the Federals escaped

Cedarville

Cedarville is located about five miles north of Front Royal at the intersection of CR 627 and US 340/US 522 just north of I-66. Nothing remains here from Jackson's day.

During Jackson's Valley Campaign, the Confederates caught up with the Federals at Cedarville. On May 24, 1862, the day after the capture of Front Royal, the Federals were overrun and their supplies captured all along what is now CR 627 from Cedarville to Middletown, then north to Newtown along what is now US 11. Jackson's cannon shells crashed into the Federals crowded on the road, whose objective was to get to the Valley Turnpike, then turn north toward Winchester. Some described the results as "carnage."

It was the capture of supplies along these roads that gave Union general Nathaniel Banks the Confederate-bestowed nickname of "Commissary" Banks.

The night before the attack, Jackson had rested at a campfire at Cedarville. He flopped down next to General Richard Taylor, son of former president Zachary Taylor. Taylor watched Jackson stare into the fire for several hours without closing his eyes. He concluded that Jackson was either praying or had fallen into a trance.

Port Republic

Port Republic lies about 12 miles southeast of Harrisonburg. It is about one mile north of the intersection of US 340 and CR 659.

Cross Keys and Port Republic were the final battles in Jackson's Valley Campaign.

A historical marker for the Battle of Cross Keys, fought on June 8, 1862, is located at the intersection of CR 679 and VA 276 eight miles southeast of Harrisonburg and six miles west of Port Republic. Though always considered a Jackson victory, Cross Keys is not truly a Jackson site, since he had nothing to do with organizing the defenses there. He may not even have visited the battlefield. If he did, it was likely late in the day. A subordinate, General Richard Ewell, who had been ordered to link his forces with Jackson's for the Valley Campaign, did all of the fighting against Union general John C. Fremont, who had been chasing Jackson's army all the way

The Cross Keys battlefield

from west of McDowell. Though his force was less than half the size of Fremont's, Ewell beat back the one-time United States presidential candidate by holding the high ground. Following Jackson's orders not to overexpose his men, Ewell refused another general's request to roll up the Federal line, which appeared to be crumbling. Ewell thus won a victory at Cross Keys but could have made it even more devastating to the Federals.

While Ewell was handling Fremont, Jackson was preparing to face General Nathaniel Banks at Port Republic. Actually, *preparing* is not an accurate word. By that point in the three-month campaign, Jackson was near exhaustion and was making basic mistakes that frightened his staff. Some historians feel that he was beginning to show the fatigue at Port Republic that would dog his performance at the upcoming Seven Days' Battles.

The most dangerous of Jackson's Port Republic mistakes was that he made his headquarters at a house at the end of the village's main street. That house was located at the junction of two rivers, and there was no bridge at his end of the street. Jackson had literally established a headquarters at one end of a box. Mistake number two was placing his supply wagons around the headquarters on high ground, where they could easily be seen. Finally, he stationed most of his

The site of Jackson's headquarters at Port Republic

army across the river, leaving few men to guard him and his wagons. Jackson's aides recognized the mistakes but did not have the nerve to point them out to him.

On June 6, Jackson was stunned to get word that his cavalry chief, General Turner Ashby, had been killed in a rear-guard fight just southeast of Harrisonburg. Ashby's body was brought to a house in Port Republic the next day and left in the front room for Jackson to pray over it.

On the same day as Cross Keys, June 8, a Union cavalry patrol burst into Port Republic as Jackson and his staff were milling around the front yard of their headquarters. The Confederates escaped the hail of bullets, Jackson pausing briefly to admonish one of his staff members for cursing as they passed the Methodist church. The house at the corner of Main Street and CR 605 is built on the foundation of the George Kemper House, Jackson's headquarters, and looks a bit like that old home. Jackson rushed down Main and past the church. He passed over what is now CR 659 and then over a covered bridge spanning the river. The approaches to the bridge are still visible. Jackson stopped on the north side of the river. Seeing a cannon battery unlimber in town, he thought he recognized the gunners as being

The Frank Kemper House, where Jackson visited the body of General Turner Ashby

from his own Rockbridge Artillery. He decided they were not when they fired a round that missed him by a few feet.

One block west of the junction of Main and CR 659 is the yellow Frank Kemper House, now the Port Republic Museum, open on Sundays only. It was to the front room of this house that Ashby's body was taken. A mock casket with a life-sized photo of Ashby is on display in the front room. Call 540-249-5689 for information about the museum.

To reach the main part of the Port Republic battlefield, drive west on CR 659 to US 340 and turn north. Go about three miles to The Coaling, a steep, small hill on which six Union cannons were placed during the battle. Jackson ordered two regiments to take the cannons. The fight for this tiny hill and those few cannons dominated the battle. More than 300 Louisianans died here, as did an untold number of Ohio troops. After the battle, Jackson rode to The Coaling and told the surviving Louisianans that from that point onward, the cannons would be used in the memory of the men who had died capturing them.

*Main Street in Port Republic, down which
Jackson barely escaped Federal capture
in June 1862*

*The site of the bridge over which Jackson
escaped at Port Republic*

The site of the White House Bridge west of Luray. Its destruction was key to slowing the Federals chasing Jackson.

Luray/Massanutten Mountain

Luray is located at the intersection of US 340 and US 211 on the east side of Massanutten Mountain. Local legend says that Jackson and some of his men slept in the caverns that currently make this a tourist town before they turned north along what is now US 340 and headed toward Front Royal. The White House Bridge, about four miles west of town on US 211, was a key to Jackson's Valley Campaign.

The White House Bridge, named for the white house on a farm on its north side, was a key to Jackson's swift attack from McDowell toward Luray, then north to Front Royal. Jackson ordered the bridge burned after he passed over it to slow any advancing Federals. The strategy worked. One Federal column had to divert for miles, giving Jackson time that he used to his advantage by setting up defenses at Port Republic.

The gap at the top of Massanutten Mountain about four miles from the White House Bridge was another key to the Valley Campaign. The mountain runs north and south from Harrisonburg to Strasburg but has only one passable gap between New Market and Luray; that gap is located where US 211 now runs. Jackson was able to use Massanutten Mountain to screen his movements from the Federals. While they were watching on the west side of the mountain for any sign of him, he was marching swiftly north on the east side to reach Front Royal.

Rude's Hill north of New Market, where Jackson developed his Valley Campaign strategy and where he met Jed Hotchkiss

New Market/Rude's Hill

New Market is on the west side of Massanutten Mountain at the junction of US 211 and US 11. Rude's Hill is 4.4 miles north of New Market on US 11.

The Strayer Hotel is located at 9286 Congress Street in New Market, on the southeast corner of the intersection of US 11 and US 211. It was from here that Jackson watched his troops heading toward the gap leading over Massanutten Mountain toward Luray.

Neighboring Rude's Hill was Jackson's field headquarters after leaving Winchester in March 1862. It was at Rude's Hill that Jackson met the man who would help him win the Valley Campaign. That man was a New York State native, Major Jed Hotchkiss. A schoolteacher by profession, Hotchkiss had a hobby of drawing maps using colored pencils to denote changes in elevation and terrain. When Jackson learned of the hobby, he instantly realized the value Hotchkiss would bring to his staff. He called Hotchkiss into his tent. "Make me a map of the valley," Jackson said.

From that point onward, Hotchkiss's maps of many valleys and roads helped build Jackson's legend. Working with civil engineer Keith Boswell, Hotchkiss never led Jackson down a wrong road.

The value of having Hotchkiss along on a campaign was proven in the Seven Days' Battles east of Richmond in late June 1862. Jackson had left Hotchkiss in the Shenandoah Valley to draw more maps, assuming there were plenty of maps of Richmond he could use. Jackson was wrong. He got lost on the outskirts of Richmond when he did not know there were two Cold Harbors, Old and New. He did not have a Hotchkiss-drawn map showing him the route to either.

Staunton

Staunton is located southwest of Harrisonburg and northwest of Waynesboro at the intersection of I-64 and I-81. During the war, it was an important railway station and transportation center.

The first time the citizens of Staunton saw V.M.I. professor Thomas Jackson was in April 1861, when he was escorting cadets to the rail station. The cadets were on their way to Richmond to train en-

This train station stands on the site of the station where Jackson entered Staunton.

The American Hotel probably served as Jackson's temporary headquarters in Staunton.

thusiastic but bumbling new recruits into the Confederate army.

When Stonewall Jackson and his men showed up in Staunton on May 4, 1862, on trains they had boarded at Mechum's River Station just west of Charlottesville, the citizens were surprised to see them. Like the Federals, the citizens had no idea where Jackson was. The latest rumor had him heading for Richmond. Now, here he was in the heart of the Shenandoah again.

Jackson spent three days in town resting his men before heading them west along what is now VA 254 toward the Alleghenies, where he joined forces with General Edward Johnson, who was facing a threat from Union general John C. Fremont.

While in Staunton, Jed Hotchkiss, Jackson's mapmaker, got to stop home at 437 East Beverly Street.

Just a block east of Hotchkiss's home, on the grounds of the Virginia School for the Deaf and Blind, Jackson reviewed the V.M.I. cadets who had been ordered to join him. He sent the ones younger than 18 home, as V.M.I. had not asked their parents' permission for them to join the army. He assigned the rest to the Stonewall Brigade. They would later return to V.M.I.

South of downtown at the corner of Middlebrook Avenue and Augusta Street is the American Hotel, which may have been Jackson's headquarters during his three days in town, as it was right across the street from the train station. The current station was built in 1902 on the same site as the one Jackson used.

To see the graves of two of Jackson's right-hand men, visit Thornrose Cemetery, located in the 1100 block of Beverly Street.

Pass the main office and park on the right. Walk up the first road leading into the cemetery, heading up the hill. Watch on the left for the grave of Major Jed Hotchkiss, the New York-born schoolteacher

Jed Hotchkiss's postwar house in Staunton

whose hobby of drawing maps allowed Jackson to get his "foot cavalry" wherever it needed to go. It was Hotchkiss's maps that helped seal the success of the Valley Campaign. It was leaving Hotchkiss behind to draw more maps of the Shenandoah Valley that contributed to Jackson's poor performance during the Seven Days' Battles near Richmond. Had Hotchkiss been along, Jackson would have at least known where he was going.

When the Federals tried to confiscate his maps after the war, Hotchkiss appealed to an old enemy, U. S. Grant, who allowed him to keep them. He later donated them to the Library of Congress, where they are still used to study the war.

From Hotchkiss's grave, head up the road into the cemetery, then turn right at the next intersecting road. Turn left at the next road. You are now on the outer road of the cemetery. Stop across from a maintenance shed on the edge of the property, then walk back into the cemetery. Watch for a large tombstone for the Lemmons family.

The grave of Jed Hotchkiss, Jackson's mapmaker, in Thornrose Cemetery in Staunton

The grave of Jackson's quartermaster, John Harman, in Staunton's Thornrose Cemetery

Turn right and look for the markers for the Harman family. One of them honors John Harman, Jackson's quartermaster.

Before the war, Harman and his brother ran a stagecoach company in Staunton that took people up and down the valley. Early in the conflict, Jackson convinced Harman to become his quartermaster, a job he apparently did quite well, though he did not like it—or Jackson—very much. In letters home, Harman sometimes threatened to quit because Jackson was always asking the impossible of him. It was Harman who had to untangle traffic jams of his wagons at river fords. After much yelling and cursing, sometimes in front of Jackson, Harman always got the wagons across. Harman was not a professional soldier, though Jackson made the mistake of treating him like one. During the Seven Days' Battles, Jackson gave Harman long verbal instructions to relay to two divisions, ordering them into a complex maneuver. By the time Harman found the division generals and tried to relay the order, he could not remember all the details. The two generals had no idea what Jackson wanted them to do, so they did nothing. Harman was blamed for the error.

From the cemetery, follow VA 254 (the Staunton-Parkersburg Turnpike), which leads west. Jackson and his troops took this vital road on the way to McDowell.

McDowell

The roadside park for Mountain House Ranger District is on US 250 about 25 miles west of Staunton. The little town of McDowell is about 35 miles west of Staunton on US 250. The battlefield, about a mile east of town, is accessible only by a strenuous climb. The Felix Hull House still stands in the village; a historical marker is on US 250 nearby.

*The site of the Mountain House, where Jackson
spent the night before the Battle of McDowell*

Jackson moved from Staunton toward McDowell in May 1862 because he wanted to stop United States general John C. Fremont from advancing on the Shenandoah Valley from the west. The lone Confederate force in the area, under General Edward Johnson, was no match for Fremont, so Jackson's only choice was to link with Johnson before Fremont could figure out what was happening.

Jackson spent the night before the Battle of McDowell at what is now the Mountain House Ranger District roadside park in a house occupied by a toll-gate keeper. From this point onward, the Confederates pushed back advance scouting units of Federals under General Robert Milroy. It slowly dawned on the Federals who was reenforcing Johnson. Jackson, who was supposed to be at least 200 miles away, had suddenly appeared in their front.

There is a parking area with an interpretive marker on the south side of US 250 east of McDowell. Park here if you care to take a 1.8-mile round-trip hike up Sitlington Hill, the primary battleground for the Battle of McDowell. Be forewarned that this hike is up the side of a small mountain. Though the walk is not dangerous, it should be undertaken only by those in good shape. Take water. If you make the trek, you'll get a good idea of how rugged this country

The view from the top of Sitlington Hill

is and what it must have been like to pull and push cannons up these mountains.

Sitlington Hill is part of Bullpasture Mountain. Its heights gave a commanding view of the valley below and were a perfect site for the placement of troops. It was here that Jackson found General Edward Johnson, the commander of Confederate forces in the area. Johnson had been given the nickname "Allegheny" by his men in honor of his continuing service in the mountains. Jackson, used to meeting unusual people and being one himself, found his match in Johnson. Johnson had a huge, beehive-shaped head and a nervous tic that made one of his eyes blink uncontrollably. He carried a large club both as a walking stick and as a symbol of authority.

Jackson decided that it was too late to start a battle on May 8, so he left Sitlington Hill after surveying the scene and headed back to his men, leaving Johnson's men in position on top of the mountain. Milroy, not willing to cede the high ground to Johnson, attacked, much to the surprise of Jackson, who was several miles away when he heard the shooting start.

The men of General William Taliaferro rushed to the defense of the Confederates holding Sitlington Hill, whose line was about to break. It was only after most of the fighting was over that Jackson

*Sitlington Hill on top of Bullpasture Mountain,
the site of heavy fighting at McDowell*

arrived with the Stonewall Brigade. That must have irked Jackson. It
was Taliaferro who, after being left in Romney, had led the way in
complaining to Richmond about Jackson just four months earlier.
Jackson had resigned over the incident but had been persuaded to
stay in the army.

McDowell was a strange battle. It was fought without any artillery at all, since the slopes were too high to haul up cannons. Jackson lost three times more men then the Federals did, which is likely
explained by the ground being so steep that the Confederates were
outlined against the evening sky.

The next day, Jackson made his headquarters in the home of
Felix Hull in the village. From there, he wrote a note to Richmond
saying only, "God blessed our arms with victory at McDowell yes-
terday." He made no mention of where Milroy and Fremont were,
no mention of losses, no mention of what he was planning to do
next, no mention of Taliaferro. It was typical Jackson.

While Jackson was writing his reports, he ordered the boys of
V.M.I. to start burying the dead. Most were laid to rest in unmarked
graves in the cemetery across from the Presbyterian church.

Jackson pursued the Federals for several days but never caught

The Felix Hull House, Jackson's temporary headquarters in McDowell

up to them to do more battle. He hoped to reach Milroy before he had a chance to reunite with the much larger force of Fremont. When he could not catch Milroy, Jackson backed off. On May 13, he started marching back toward Staunton to reunite his forces with those of Richard Ewell.

Jackson would subsequently rush to Front Royal, then to Winchester, then to Harpers Ferry, then back down to Port Republic, winning victory on each battlefield.

Warm Springs/Hot Springs/ Bath Alum Springs/ Rockbridge Alum Springs

All of these mineral springs are located close to each other about an hour's drive northwest of Lexington. Most of them are along or near VA 39. Warm Springs is just west of the intersection of VA 39 and US 220 about 45 miles west of Lexington. Hot Springs is on US 220 about five miles south of Warm Springs. What was once Bath Alum Springs is on VA 39 about 10 miles east of Warm Springs. Rockbridge Alum Springs is about six miles south of the town of Goshen. It may be reached by taking CR 780 south from Goshen. The road becomes CR 486. Turn right at the intersection with CR 633 and look for the entrance.

Stonewall Jackson loved nothing more than taking a nice, relaxing bath.

That sounds like an unusual statement about a man who won fame fighting Federals on Virginia and Maryland battlefields, but it is true. Jackson loved visiting what today would be called health spas. All his life, he was troubled—or thought he was troubled—by poor digestion, weak vision, bad circulation, and ill health in general.

In the 1840s and 1850s, one of the popular health treatments was to drink and soak in mineral water, whether it be hot, warm, or cold. The regimen of "taking the waters" both externally and internally was called hydrotherapy by its proponents, who usually recommended a healthy dose of exercise in addition to the water. Sometimes, the treatments bordered on the bizarre. One of Jackson's "doctors" suggested he wear a wet shirt next to his body.

Jackson became a devotee of hydrotherapy in 1849 while stationed at Fort Hamilton, New York. Over the next 11 years, he visited numerous springs in New York, Vermont, Massachusetts, and Virginia. While his writings seem to indicate that he preferred the mixture of waters and exercise that was practiced in the North, Jackson also enjoyed the springs closer to his adopted home of Lexington.

One spring where ordinary tourists can "take the waters" is Warm Springs, also called the Jefferson Pools. Here, men and women still use separate bathhouses, just as they did before the Civil War. The water is crystal clear and lukewarm. Baths were $12 at the time of

Inside the Jefferson Pools, which Jackson first used in 1851

The men's bathhouse at the Jefferson Pools in Warm Springs

this writing. Dressing rooms are provided, and there is an attendant inside each bathhouse. This may be the only place in the world where a tourist can experience the same soothing springs that first Thomas Jackson and later Robert E. Lee enjoyed. An analysis of the minerals in the water at Warm Springs is posted on the wall. The land surrounding the springs was a campground for V.M.I. cadets. Jackson led them on a summer march when he arrived in 1851. Not surprisingly, the route of the march went to several of the springs in which Jackson wanted to bathe.

Jackson also visited Hot Springs, which has developed into a wealthy tourist resort today. Healing Springs, just past Hot Springs, was also a Jackson stop. It is now part of Hot Springs.

What was once Bath Alum Springs is located on private property marked by a white fence along VA 39. This was also a campground for V.M.I. cadets and Jackson. The springs are no longer open to the public.

Rockbridge Alum Springs—which Jackson proclaimed the second-finest springs resort in Virginia, after White Sulphur Springs (now located in West Virginia)—is known today as Young Life, a Christian youth camp. In its heyday in the 1850s, more than 500 guests could stay at Rockbridge Alum Springs. During a visit here in 1852, Jackson wrote to his sister that he had to share a bed with another guest, and that there were four guests to a room. Board was $10 a week, which was pretty steep in those days. Still, Jackson liked his stay. He wrote, "This water I consider is the water of waters. I have not heard of a single person who is dissatisfied." Robert E. Lee and his family were occasional visitors here after he moved to Lexington in 1865. Rockbridge Alum Springs is not open to tourists, but arrangements can be made for church and business groups during the nine months

An original building at Rockbridge Alum Springs

The restored springhouse at Rockbridge Alum Springs

An original guest cottage at Rockbridge Alum Springs

of the year when it is not used as a summer resort by Young Life. The springs no longer flow here, but several of the original buildings still stand and are in use. Call 540-997-9276 for information.

*The Stonewall Jackson House
in Lexington*

Lexington

*Lexington, the final home and resting place of both Stonewall
Jackson and Robert E. Lee, is located at the upper (or southern)
end of the Shenandoah Valley at the intersection of I-81 and
US 60.*

In the spring of 1851, Thomas J. Jackson—a lieutenant who also
carried the brevet, or honorary, rank of major for his heroism in the
Mexican War of 1846-47—resigned from the United States Army.
What brought him to Lexington, a town he had never seen, was the
offer of a professorship of natural and experimental philosophy (what
we now call physics) at Virginia Military Institute. Major Jackson—
who used his brevet title at V.M.I., though he was out of the army—
did double duty at the school. He taught physics, a subject in which

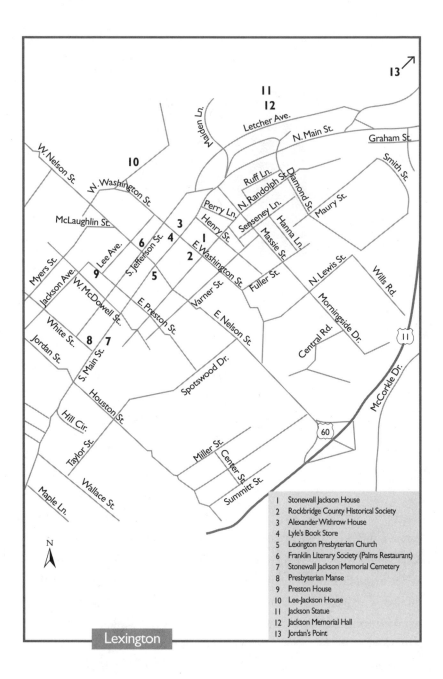

1	Stonewall Jackson House
2	Rockbridge County Historical Society
3	Alexander Withrow House
4	Lyle's Book Store
5	Lexington Presbyterian Church
6	Franklin Literary Society (Palms Restaurant)
7	Stonewall Jackson Memorial Cemetery
8	Presbyterian Manse
9	Preston House
10	Lee-Jackson House
11	Jackson Statue
12	Jackson Memorial Hall
13	Jordan's Point

Lexington

IN THE FOOTSTEPS OF STONEWALL JACKSON

The traveling desk Jackson gave his father-in-law, Dr. George Junkin as a wedding appreciation gift is owned by the Rockbridge County Historical Society.

he had never before instructed students, and artillery tactics, a skill that had earned him fame in Mexico.

Jackson quickly proved a poor teacher. He had no charisma, no ability to connect with young students. Naturally reserved from his upbringing as an orphan raised by uncles, Jackson memorized the lessons he was to teach each day, then recited them to the students. When a cadet didn't understand his meaning, Jackson simply recited the same passage of the lesson again. Given his poor teaching methods and his odd, long-legged, big-footed, staring-at-the-ground gait, it is easy to see how cadets thought him eccentric. Some began calling him "Tom Fool" Jackson.

It was in the fall of 1852 that the young professor's thoughts turned to love. In the year and a half he had been in Lexington, he had become friends with Dr. George Junkin, the president of Washington College. Dr. and Mrs. Junkin had two daughters, Margaret (or "Maggie") and Elinor (or "Ellie"). Margaret was four years older than Jackson and thus a little out of his reach, but Ellie was younger and eligible. The two became friends as Sunday-school teachers.

One day, Jackson was talking to his Mexican War friend Daniel

Harvey Hill, a professor at Washington College. Jackson complained that he felt odd around Ellie. Hill laughed and told him he was in love. That had never occurred to Jackson.

In August 1853, Jackson and Ellie were married in the Junkin home. They lived in the north wing of the house until October 22, 1854, when Ellie died in childbirth.

Jackson was devastated. For a while, he contemplated suicide. His friends worried that he would sink into madness in his grief.

In time, Jackson got over Ellie's death with the help of her sister, Maggie. Historians have speculated that the two may have fallen in love despite their age difference. If so, it was a love that was never fulfilled. The laws of the Presbyterian Church forbade a relationship between a widower and his dead wife's sister.

Jackson was ready to move on with his life. He remembered the sisters of D. H. Hill's wife, the Morrison girls, who had visited the Hill family in Lexington in the summer of 1852. Jackson, already engaged to Ellie, had treated them like his own sisters and had no romantic interest in them. But now, looking for love, he remembered one sister in particular, Mary Anna, called "Anna." Jackson sent a letter to her home near Davidson, North Carolina, reminding her of the interesting times they had spent together during her visits to Lexington. The Morrisons thought it odd that a man who had not seen Anna for nearly four years was writing.

Just before Christmas 1856, Jackson literally showed up on the Morrisons' doorstep asking to see Anna. The two apparently became engaged in just a few days, though they had never been on a formal date. They were married on July 16, 1857.

When they arrived in Lexington after their honeymoon, they first moved into the Lexington Hotel, then into an unnamed rooming house. On April 30, 1858, Anna gave birth to a baby, Mary Graham, who lived only six weeks.

In the fall of 1858, Jackson and Anna bought a house. Finally, Jackson had a loving wife and a home he could call his own. The orphan boy was happy. He would live in the house until leaving for war on April 21, 1861, after which he would never see it again.

The Stonewall Jackson House, located at 8 East Washington Street, is a mandatory stop for anyone interested in Jackson's life. Purchased as a "fixer-upper," this was the only house Jackson ever owned. He made it into a loving, if practical, home. Jackson, thought rigid by his friends and students, would sometimes hide behind the door and leap out to smother his wife with kisses. Much of the furniture in the house came from New York, reflecting Jackson's taste for quality things he didn't think he could purchase locally. One room was reserved for Jackson's study. Here, he would face the wall, standing up at his desk, and memorize his lessons. In back outside the house is evidence of another of Jackson's passions—a vegetable garden. Jackson subscribed to various gardening magazines and often talked about how much he loved to dig in the dirt and watch things grow. For information on the Stonewall Jackson House, call 540-463-2552.

Across the street is the Rockbridge County Historical Society. Inside is a sign-in desk that was used by the Franklin Literary Society, a debating club that helped Jackson become a member of local society. Viewable upon request is a fine traveling desk that Jackson had made as a gift to his first father-in-law, Dr. George Junkin, after marrying his daughter. For information about the historical society, call 540-464-1058.

Located at the northwest corner of Washington and Main is the Alexander Withrow House, which now serves as a bed-and-breakfast. In Jackson's day, it was a bank. He served as a director and was also an investor.

On the southeast corner is the third courthouse that has stood

The sign-in desk for the Franklin Literary Society, is on display at the Rockbridge County Historical Society.

The Palms Restaurant in Lexington, former home of the Franklin Literary Society, where Jackson first tried his public speaking skills

on this site. Jackson once got into an argument with an ardent secessionist at a previous building here.

On the west side of the street at 15 Main is the Rockbridge Building, which now houses a record store. In Jackson's day, this was a bookstore owned by a friend, John Lyle, who helped introduce Jackson to Presbyterianism.

A half-block north on the east side of Main is the McCampbell Inn, now a bed-and-breakfast. The central portion of this building

*The Alexander Withrow House in Lexington,
once a bank in which Jackson invested*

*The site of Lyle's Book Store in
Lexington. A favorite haunt of Jackson's*

was the hotel where Jackson and Anna first stayed when they returned from their honeymoon.

Jefferson Street runs parallel to Main Street one block to the
west. On the corner of Jefferson and Nelson Streets is the Palms
Restaurant. The bottom part of this building was salvaged after
the top half burned in 1915. The building once housed the Franklin

Lexington Presbyterian Church is being rebuilt after a 2000 fire.

Literary Society, where leading citizens—Jackson among them—went to debate topics of the day. A cornerstone with *F.L.S.* carved into it is visible in the courtyard of the restaurant.

On the corner of Nelson and Main is Lexington Presbyterian Church, which has been undergoing extensive rebuilding since a fire in 2000. This is where Jackson worshiped every Sunday and where he ran a controversial Sunday school for black adults and children. Several times, he got into arguments with local citizens, who pointed out that it was illegal to teach blacks to read, which is what Jackson was doing. Jackson ignored his critics and the law. He knew the Lord wanted everyone—black and white, slave and free—to read His Word.

The Stonewall Jackson Memorial Cemetery is two blocks south of Lexington Presbyterian Church at Main and McDowell Streets. Immediately to the right upon entering the cemetery is the grave of Major Sandie Pendleton, one of Jackson's best aides, who was killed in 1864. Several graves farther east lies Dr. William S. White, the pastor who taught Jackson how to become a Presbyterian and who officiated at his funeral. Not far from White is John Letcher, the wartime governor and friend of Jackson's who barged into Secretary of

The grave of Lieutenant Colonel Sandie Pendleton, the Jackson aide who was killed more than a year after the general

The grave of Governor John Letcher, Jackson's close friend who got him to rescind his resignation from the Confederate army

The grave of the Reverend W. S. White, the pastor who taught Jackson how to be a Presbyterian and who preached his funeral

War Judah Benjamin's office enraged that Jackson had resigned from the army after Benjamin had rescinded an order of Jackson's. The first fenced family plot to the left of the walkway is that of the Junkins. Here rests Elinor Junkin Jackson, the first wife of Thomas. Their stillborn son was placed in her arms and buried in the same casket. Jackson was first buried in front of the Junkin plot. His original tombstone is still in place. Photographs from the 1870s show young women in mourning around this tombstone. A statue of Jackson was erected just east of his original grave in 1891. His body was subsequently moved to lie beneath the statue. The remains of Anna and their daughter, Julia, are there, too.

White Street lies just south of McDowell. At 6 White Street is the Presbyterian manse where Dr. William S. White often met with Jackson to teach him what it meant to be of that faith.

Preston Street is one block north of McDowell. At 110 West Preston is the former home of Jackson friend John Preston and his wife, Margaret Junkin Preston, the older sister of Ellie.

Lee Avenue leads north off Preston Street to the campus of

The original grave site of Jackson
He was later moved under the statue.

Jackson burial site in Lexington

The grave of Ellie Junkin
Jackson, Jackson's first wife, who
died in childbirth. Their
stillborn baby was put into her
arms inside the casket.

The Presbyterian manse in
Lexington, where Jackson
studied to become a Presbyterian

The home of Margaret Junkin Preston, Jackson's first sister-in-law, who became his best friend after his wife's death

Washington and Lee University—Washington College in Jackson's day. The first home visitors will encounter on the sidewalk leading through campus is the Lee House, built to Robert E. Lee's specifications. The second home is the Lee-Jackson House, occupied in 1851 by the Junkin family. After Jackson married Ellie, the couple lived in the north wing of the house. Following her death, Jackson moved back to the V.M.I. barracks. The Lees lived in this same home when they first moved to Lexington, making it the only house once occupied by both Robert E. Lee and Stonewall Jackson.

Just to the north is the campus of Virginia Military Institute. As visitors round a corner, they will see the main barracks, where four red-wheeled cannons stand in front of a statue. At the base of the statue are the buried bones of Little Sorrel, who was actually called "Fancy" most of the time by Jackson. The statue itself is unusual. Though it supposedly shows Jackson at Chancellorsville, he never

The Lee-Jackson House at Washington and Lee University Jackson and wife Ellie lived in the north wing.

The V.M.I. Barracks

Jackson statue in front of the V. M. I. barraacks
He actually never wore the style of hat depicted.

Matthew, Mark, Luke, and John, the four six-pounder cannons Jackson used when he first left for war

wore the type of hat depicted. He was definitely wearing his favorite forage hat on the day he was shot.

As for the four six-pounder cannons, bright red wheels are not considered to be a very smart idea in combat, since artillery is supposed to blend into the countryside. But the wheels were painted that way so citizens watching the gunners drill would know they were the proud cadets of V.M.I.. The guns were actually smaller than standard military six-pounders by more than 300 pounds. They were specially designed so the cadets could move them around the field by hand, rather than using horses. These guns, nicknamed Matthew, Mark, Luke, and John, were the four cannons taken to war by Jackson's first chief of artillery, William Nelson Pendleton. Pendleton commanded them in Colonel Jackson's first skirmish at Falling Waters in June 1861. Since the guns were so small, they were soon sent back to Lexington. These are the only cannons in existence confirmed as having been commanded by Jackson.

When he was single, Jackson lived and taught in the barracks behind the statue. In 1863, his body lay in state in a lecture room here. The V.M.I. barracks are off-limits to visitors.

To the right of the statue is the V.M.I. Museum. Inside are several precious Jackson artifacts, including his hat, the raincoat he was wearing on the night he was shot, and the preserved skin of Little Sorrel.

The sleeve of the raincoat shows the damage done by the volley that felled Jackson. The raincoat has an interesting story. Following Jackson's death, it was discarded and its connection to the general forgotten. It was later purchased by a soldier who looked at the battle damage to the coat, then looked for a name. He found Jackson's. The coat eventually went to Jackson's widow and her daughter, who donated it to V.M.I.

Little Sorrel is shown as he was in life—smaller than a horse one might expect a five-foot-eleven-inch general to be riding. Jackson liked to have his stirrups up high, which created what looked like an awkward riding position to everyone but him. Jackson once switched horses with an aide. Both of them had to stop, Jackson to adjust his stirrups higher and the aide to put his lower. The aide said

Little Sorrell, Jackson's most famous war horse, survived the general and was buried within two miles of him.

that if he had not lowered his stirrups, he would have hit himself in the chin with his knees. Jackson's riding style may have come from his youthful days at Jackson's Mill, where he was a jockey for his uncle's racehorses. As he grew up, he became too large to be a jockey, but he must have liked the high stirrups of his racing days.

For information about the V.M.I. Museum, call 540-464-7334.

A couple of other Jackson-related sites lie near the Lexington Visitors Center, located at 106 East Washington Street.

A few blocks to the east are a residential area and the headquarters of the Sigma Nu fraternity. In Jackson's day, this hill was the "colored cemetery." The graves were later supposed to be removed and transferred to another cemetery, but historians have speculated that the contractor hired to do the work failed to carry it out. Jackson's elderly housekeeper, Amy, and his faithful servant, Jim Lewis, who died not long after the war, were buried here.

One block north of the Lexington Visitors Center is a parking lot for a laundromat. Jackson's strangest business venture—a tannery in which he owned an interest—was located here. Details on the tannery are skimpy. If it was a true tannery, where animal hides were boiled and separated from the bodies, then the smell must have

The site of Jackson's tannery, less than a block from his home in Lexington

been tremendous—hardly the sort of thing that someone would put on the edge of a populated area. It seems more likely that the operation was some sort of finishing shop, a place where hides were softened and the odor was less offensive.

Two final sites are on the outskirts of Lexington.

Jordan's Point is a small city park located on the southwest side of US 11 before it passes over the Maury River north of downtown Lexington. Jackson's body was brought here by riverboat, to a stone dock almost covered by vines. He was transported to the V.M.I. bar-

Dam at Jordan's Point in Lexington, Virginia

The stone-wall dock where Jackson's body was unloaded at Jordan's Point

racks by cadets. There is a little irony at this spot. Jackson's second military mission was to destroy Dam Number Five on the Potomac River early in 1861. His last stop on the Maury River was just below a dam that looks exactly like Dam Number Five.

What was once Jackson's farm is on the east side of town. Quarry Lane is located off US 60 just past US 11 Bypass. The "country farm" that Jackson cultivated from 1859 to 1861 was about 200 yards behind the Taco Bell restaurant on the left. Here, Jackson grew all sorts of small crops, more for the pure enjoyment of it than anything else. He usually had three of his slaves working this plot of land because they, too, liked growing things. The entire farm is now a rock quarry. Nothing grows on Jackson's farm today.

The quarry that was once Jackson's farm outside Lexington

What is left of the Marshall, *the riverboat that took Jackson's body to Lexington*

Lynchburg

Lynchburg is in southwest Virginia at the intersection of US 29 and US 460. Riverside Park is located 1.8 miles north of downtown at 2240 Rivermont Avenue, beside the James River.

One of the sadder relics of Stonewall Jackson's life and death lies decaying in a Lynchburg city park, surrounded by a chain-link fence that does nothing to protect it from the elements.

On his deathbed, Jackson agreed with his wife that he would be buried in Lexington, his adopted hometown. Since no train line ran near Lexington, it was decided that his body would be transported from Richmond to Lynchburg (the closest rail stop), then on to Lexington by riverboat.

On May 13, 1863, Jackson's body arrived in Lynchburg, awaited by a crowd of mourners. That night, a church service was held in his honor. The next morning, the body, accompanied by Mrs. Jackson, was put on a canal boat called the *Marshall* and started west on the James, pulled by a mule team. Eventually, the boat was pulled up the north fork of the James (what is now called the Maury River) to a landing just short of a dam north of Lexington.

Once it left Jackson's body, the *Marshall* returned to service on the James. It may have been the same canal boat that took Robert E. Lee's family to Lexington in the late fall of 1865, after Lee took the job as president of Washington College. That boat has been described in accounts as being owned by the president of the canal-boat company, while the *Marshall* has been described as the "queen" of that company's line. It seems likely that the president of the company would have used his best boat to transport Lee's family.

The iron keel of the *Marshall*, the last public conveyance Jackson ever took, now rests and rusts in the back of this Lynchburg city park, far out of sight of a public that likely doesn't know it even exists.

Mechum's River Station

Mechum's River Station no longer exists as a rail stop. The station was located down Mechum's Depot Lane just west of US 250 and VA 240 about six miles west of Charlottesville and very near the Mechum's River. The building on the site now is not of Civil War vintage.

Mechum's River Station is where Jackson's troops boarded the train to Staunton on their way to McDowell in May 1862. It is also where Jackson sneaked aboard a special train heading east in late June 1862. That train took him to his first meeting with Lee to plan what would become the Seven Days' Campaign.

In mid-June 1862, Stonewall Jackson was an exhausted man.

*Mechum's River Station, where Jackson's men
boarded trains for the Battle of McDowell*

Since March, he had been riding up and down the Shenandoah Valley
keeping several Federal armies at bay, chasing and being chased. For
weeks, he had been surviving on what sleep he could snatch a few
hours at a time under trees and along fence rows. Some generals
operated out of houses, but Jackson often worked out of his tent or
even his saddle. He ate when he could.

Jackson's private nature was partly to blame for his exhaustion.
In his view, his generals existed only to follow his orders, not as
sounding boards for his ideas. He formulated each battle plan in his
head, rarely writing anything down and almost never telling his generals in advance what he wanted them to do the next day, or sometimes even the next hour. He kept his own counsel, something that
must have been highly stressful physically and mentally.

When Lee secretly asked for Jackson's help in fighting back
McClellan, who was edging closer to Richmond, he had no idea how
close to collapse Jackson was. Jackson's staff members knew he was
so tired he was almost ill, but they said nothing to Lee. Jackson didn't
say anything either. This silence cost the lives of hundreds of Confederates at the Seven Days' Battles and rubbed some of the polish off
Jackson's image.

Jackson told only one aide—Major Robert Dabney, a clergyman who had no military background—about Lee's request that he move his forces toward Richmond. Everyone else was left in the dark, including Jackson's generals. On June 19, Jackson boarded a train heading east from Mechum's River Station to confer with Lee. He made it only to Gordonsville, where he had to stop to check out rumors that a large Federal force was moving on that location. Precious time was thus lost. It was not until June 22 that Jackson and Dabney boarded a train leaving Gordonsville and headed east toward Richmond. They next stopped at Fredericks Hall, located about 40 miles north of Richmond.

CR 633 in Grottoes, the road Jackson's men took to Brown's Gap, then to Mechum's River Station

Brown's Gap

Brown's Gap, elevation 2,600 feet, is located at Milepost 83 on Skyline Drive.

The fire road that crosses Brown's Gap—called Madison Run Fire Road (CR 663) on the west and Brown's Gap Fire Road (CR 629) on the east—was used by Jackson to get his men south to Mechum's River Station, where they boarded trains that would take them to McDowell during the Valley Campaign in May 1862. Jackson's men also camped in this area after moving east following the fighting at Port Republic several weeks later.

CR 663 can be accessed from the town of Grottoes on US 340 in the Shenandoah Valley, but just as on top of the mountain, it is maintained as a fire road and is closed to traffic. Hiking Jackson's route up and down the mountain is allowed.

Gordonsville Presbyterian Church, where Jackson's pew is preserved

Gordonsville

Gordonsville lies about 20 miles northeast of Charlottesville at the junction of US 15 and US 33. The Exchange Hotel Museum is an excellent small-town museum that interprets Civil War medicine. Jackson used the hotel on several occasions when it served as a train stop. Call 540-832-2944 for information.

Gordonsville and nearby Orange Court House were two centers of troop activity during most of the war, since they were located deep in the heart of Virginia and along rail lines. This area was also a good, central location from which to move in response to any Northern threat. Lee brought the Army of Northern Virginia to the fields between the two towns to refit and rest.

It was from the train stop at the Exchange Hotel—located where US 33 crosses the tracks southeast of the center of Gordonsville—that Jackson's army boarded the train in mid-June 1862 to continue moving from the Shenandoah Valley to the Seven Days' Battles around Richmond. And it was at the same stop that Jackson's body was unloaded from one train and placed on another headed toward Lynchburg, where it was transferred to a canal boat to begin its final journey for burial in Lexington.

While in town, Jackson attended Gordonsville Presbyterian Church, located on US 33 about half a mile north of the Exchange Hotel Museum. The church has preserved the hard wooden bench on which Jackson habitually slept while sitting upright during services. The bench is right inside the front door.

An ice cream restaurant is located at the traffic circle where US 33 meets US 15. It was in a house on this spot that Jackson made his headquarters during his time in Gordonsville. The house of the Presbyterian minister was nearby. Though Jackson slept through religious services, he liked to talk over religion with ministers at their homes.

Orange Court House/Liberty Mills

Orange (formerly Orange Court House) lies about 10 miles north of Gordonsville at the junction of US 15 and VA 20. Liberty Mills is located on VA 231 less than a mile north of VA 20. It is about five miles west of Orange.

Like neighboring Gordonsville, Orange Court House was a center of troop activity during most of the war, thanks to its location and its access to rail lines. One Jackson site in Orange Court House that still exists is the Mayhurst Inn, a bed-and-breakfast located at 12460 Mayhurst Lane. Jackson spent at least one night here as a guest of the Willis family before the Battle of Cedar Mountain in 1862.

Pause at the bridge over the Rapidan River when you visit Liberty Mills. It was here at an unnamed site—simply called "Ewell's headquarters" in historical accounts—that Jackson showed a petulant side to his character. That trait was certainly nothing new to people who knew him. But Jackson may have also shown a dishonest side, which was unfamiliar.

On August 5, 1862, Jackson convened a court-martial at Liberty Mills for General Richard Garnett for dereliction of duty at the Battle of Kernstown on March 23. Garnett, in command of the Stonewall Brigade on the date in question, had pulled his men back from the action when they began to run out of ammunition. Jackson, leading more men to the front to reenforce Garnett, had been livid. He determined that Garnett should have stayed in position even if it meant facing the Federals with bayonets.

Jackson went into the proceedings with no one on his side to prove his charges. Indeed, all of the regimental colonels in the brigade backed Garnett's version of the story, that they would have been slaughtered had Garnett not pulled them back. Garnett cross-examined Jackson, charging that he, the general in charge of the battle, actually made the mistakes that led to the fix in which the Stonewall Brigade found itself. Jackson vigorously denied making some statements that Garnett attributed to him. The next day, Jackson ended the court-martial before it could render a verdict, citing news that the Federals were moving south and had already reached Culpeper, about 15 miles away.

Garnett never got the satisfaction of having his case decided one way or the other. Jackson, perhaps sensing he was losing, never called the court-martial back into session, even in the relatively calm days after the return of the army from Sharpsburg in September 1862. When Jackson was killed in May 1863, Garnett felt his honor had been tarnished by a man who had become a martyr.

Garnett was killed on July 3, 1863, leading his brigade from his horse on the Pettigrew-Pickett-Trimble Assault at Gettysburg. Some historians have speculated that Garnett rode his horse in order to show he was not afraid to make himself a conspicuous target. That discounts the fact that other officers also rode their horses on that charge. If Garnett had a death wish, he shared it with other men.

Cedar Mountain

The ground where the Battle of Cedar Mountain was fought lies along US 15 about 11 miles north of Orange and about five miles southwest of Culpeper. Cedar Mountain is also called Slaughter Mountain. Slow down when you approach the area and look for a red-brick house on the east side of US 15. This was Jackson's headquarters during the battle. Turn left on CR 691 (Carver School Road), drive to a stop sign, then turn right on CR 657 (General Winder Road), the original road that led into Culpeper. Drive nearly a mile, then pull over at the marker where the road (now called Crittenden Lane) curves back to the right.

When Jackson heard that Federals under John Pope were marching south toward Culpeper, then on toward Orange Court House, he decided to hit them head on, rather than to wait for them to come to him. But as was typical of Stonewall, he did not tell his subordinate generals what he intended to do. His minimal orders gave the general direction in which to march. Jackson did not even tell A. P. Hill, a division commander, of a change in marching orders, then was livid when Hill was not marching according to the orders Jackson had not issued.

On August 9, 1862, Jackson's advance bumped into Pope's advance. Jackson was pleased when he learned who was in command of that Union advance—Nathaniel Banks, the Massachusetts political general Jackson had defeated in the Valley Campaign back in May and June.

The battle started as an artillery duel, Jackson's guns setting up on the bottom slope of Cedar Mountain east of US 15. The infantry filed in a line extending across where the highway runs today; no road existed there at the time. Jackson himself rode to the front near the mountain and was almost hit by an exploding Federal artillery shell.

Midway through the afternoon, Jackson got word that his extreme left was in danger of collapsing after his hand-picked leader of the Stonewall Brigade, General Charles Winder, was blown apart by

Jackson's temporary headquarters at Cedar Mountain

Spot where Jackson rallied his troops at Cedar Mountain in August 1862

an artillery ball. Jackson came rushing across what is now US 15 and down what is now Crittenden Lane to the area near this marker to rally his troops. Gunfire raged all around him as the Federals drew closer. Jackson, normally a calm, detached commander, started shouting for his men to rally. In one hand, he grabbed a battle flag. In the other, he waved his sword, scabbard and all. He had so rarely drawn his saber that it had rusted into its scabbard.

Jackson won the Battle of Cedar Mountain, but just barely. Banks, who led what was simply an advance force, had half the men Jackson did, yet he stopped Jackson dead in his tracks. Jackson had not prepared his brigadiers for battle and had been slow to move them into position once the battle was under way.

Pope felt pretty good about the battle. He figured he had done well to stop Jackson. But then he made a tactical mistake. He began edging south toward Orange Court House. Soon, his entire army was between the Rappahannock and Rapidan Rivers. He put himself in a natural bottleneck.

When Lee saw the trap Pope had created for himself, he tried to form a battle plan to seal off one end of the bottle with Confederate cavalry. Jackson and Longstreet would then push into the head of the bottle. If the plan worked, Pope would be crushed. However, a copy of the order outlining the plan was lost by the cavalry, and Pope soon pulled himself out of the trap. It was while looking for a way to get back at Pope that Lee developed the idea of having Jackson march around his flank, which led to Second Manassas about three weeks after Cedar Mountain.

The battlefield at Cedar Mountain looks much as it did in 1862, except that US 15 now crosses it.

Chancellorsville

The site of Jackson's last battle is about 10 miles directly west of Fredericksburg via VA 3. Admission to this National Park Service site also covers visits to the battlefields at Fredericksburg and Spotsylvania. The National Park Service visitor center includes a museum. If you will be visiting Ellwood, the site of the burial of Jackson's arm, on a day that it is not open to the public, secure a parking pass and directions from the desk. The route of Jackson's flank march is well marked and easily passable except after heavy, sustained rains; the road is gravel most of the way. Call 540-373-6122 for information about the National Park Service sites.

The Battle of Chancellorsville was the result of a very good idea Union general Joseph Hooker had in April and May 1863. He wanted to march west up the Rappahannock, then cross the river to get on the same side as Lee, so the Confederates could no longer use the river as a defensive position as they had in December 1862, when General Ambrose Burnside commanded the Union army. Once on the south side of the river, Hooker would have two options. He could attack Lee from the west, which would put Lee in a difficult position, since his trenches ran east and west and his army was facing north. Or Lee would be forced to attack Hooker in the open, but only after Hooker had time to dig trenches.

What Hooker did not count on was a full-scale assault by Jackson's forces on May 1. The Confederates rushed Hooker's line even though Jackson had barely ascertained its strength. Jackson hit Hooker so hard that Hooker pulled his troops back, more out of surprise and fear than out of a grand design to lure the Confederates.

Hooker then shifted into a defensive mode. Lee and Jackson conferred about what to do to get at Hooker. Jackson was of the opinion that Hooker would try to figure a way out of his predicament. Lee was convinced that Hooker was right where he wanted to be, in trenches awaiting a Confederate attack.

The Confederates were in their own fix. Lee had left only 10,000 men back in Fredericksburg to make it look like he was still there. If the Federals on the north side of the river figured out that they were facing only a skeleton force on the south side, they would cross the river and be in Lee's rear. Lee's men would be between the jaws of two larger forces.

That night, at the corner of CR 610 (Old Plank Road) and the Furnace Road southeast of where the visitor center now stands, Lee and Jackson sat on some empty cracker boxes trying to figure out how to get at Hooker. This was not a safe area. A sniper saw the two generals and flung a few rounds their way. They simply moved out of range.

Lee and Jackson had sent out their engineering officers to check the Federal defenses when General J. E. B. Stuart rode up with exciting news. Stuart's scouts had discovered that Hooker's extreme right flank was "in the air," meaning it was not anchored to anything

The site of the last meeting between Lee and Jackson

difficult to attack, such as the Rappahannock River, as the left flank was. In fact, the Federals on the far right flank were not even dug into trenches. They were merely camped in the open, not suspecting any attack on their end of the battlefield. But when the two engineering officers sent out by Lee and Jackson returned, they had discouraging news. The Union left and center were impregnable. Lee knew then that he had to attack Hooker's right flank. It was the only option.

Jackson asked local people if there were roads that led to the Federal right flank. There were. Jackson's mapmaker, Major Jed Hotchkiss, figured that the roundabout route was about 12 miles but that it might be completed in one day's march. Lee casually asked how many troops Jackson thought he should take on the march.

"My whole corps" came the reply.

Lee didn't gasp, but he might have. Jackson was talking about taking 28,000 troops, which would leave Lee with 14,000 men to face Hooker's 70,000. That was not even counting the 30,000 or so Federals back in Fredericksburg facing the 10,000 Confederates desperately trying to look like 50,000. If Hooker decided to rush out of his entrenchments in an all-out assault, there was little doubt that he would roll right over Lee's remaining forces and probably even kill or capture the general of the Army of Northern Virginia.

Lee did not hesitate. He approved Jackson's plan.

Somewhere in this historic area was a tree on which Jackson's sword was leaning. Somehow, without warning, the sword clattered to the ground, as if pushed by an unseen force. The officers in attendance glanced at each other. Since the days of the Crusades, a fallen sword has been considered an omen of bad luck. If Jackson knew of the legend, he made no mention of it.

The next morning, May 2, Jackson and Lee had their last meeting. Lee was standing on the ground, and Jackson was mounted. No one heard their last words together. Jackson pointed down the road.

If you care to follow the route of Jackson's flank march, drive down Furnace Road to Catharine Furnace. From there, National Park

Jackson Flank March Road at Chancellorsville

Stream crossing Jackson Flank March Road, from which Jackson's men filled their canteens at Chancellorsville

Service signs mark the original route for the next 12 miles. Most of the route is gravel. From the intersection of Brock Road (CR 613) and Old Plank Road (CR 621), Jackson rode up to what is now VA 3 to check his progress. It was there that he expected to attack. From the intersection of Old Plank Road and Plank Road, Jackson could see right into the Federal camp. He had not yet gone far enough. He turned back around and continued to lead his men to where Brock Road intersects VA 3 today. There, he was finally past the Federal right flank.

Jackson swung his 28,000 men in a wide arc to face them east in a line more than a mile long. When all the troops were in place just west of Wilderness Church, Jackson gave a quiet order to General Robert Rodes: "You may move your men forward."

It was after five o'clock in the afternoon. Jackson knew he had to launch an all-out surprise attack that would start the Federals running and would keep them running all night.

The Confederates smashed into the Union's 11th Corps, made up principally of German immigrants who had been forced into service with the promise of later citizenship. Most of that corps broke and ran to the rear, just as Jackson had hoped. The attack worked so well that the once-orderly Confederate line began to fall apart, as one part would surge forward while another hung back to deal with some enemy or obstacle.

Darkness soon fell, yet Jackson still pressed his men forward into the moonlight. At around nine o'clock, Jackson and his staff officers and couriers rode northeast up Mountain Road (just east of where the visitor center now stands) to see where the front was. In effect, the general in charge of the entire attack was now riding scout in front of his lines; the army he commanded was in back of him. Jackson was searching for where the Federal line was, something that scouts were expected to do. More importantly, neither he nor his aides told the nervous Confederates entrenched along the road what they were doing. No one in the front regiments imagined that their general would be riding in front of them.

Jackson rode for several hundred yards, then stopped to listen to the sounds of Federals cutting down trees to make breastworks. He turned around and was coming back down Mountain Road (which parallels today's VA 3) when a single shot rang out. Then more ragged volleys were fired from two different Confederate regiments, whose men were reacting on instinct to riders coming from the direction of the Federals.

The volleys instantly killed four riders. Jackson was hit three times—in the left arm and shoulder and the palm of the right hand. He was pulled to the ground just east of where the visitor center stands. Within a few minutes, he was moved to near where the present-day marker is located. Stretcher bearers then tried to carry Jackson west toward safety. At least twice, he was dropped to the

What is left of Mountain Road, down which Jackson rode to his wounding

This is the first monument to Jackson's wounding at Chancellorsville

This monument marks the spot where Jackson was first treated at Chancellorsville

The site where Jackson's arm is buried at Ellwood

ground when shells landed nearby. Jackson was taken to an ambulance, which transferred him to a field hospital set up near the Wilderness Tavern, located close to where VA 3 and VA 20 intersect today. There, his arm was amputated. It was sent across the road for burial in the Lacy family cemetery at Ellwood, a house that would figure prominently in the Wilderness Campaign.

Within a few hours, Jackson was loaded on an ambulance and sent to Guinea Station. If you care to follow that route, take CR 613 south from VA 3 through Spotsylvania Court House. South of the town, turn left on CR 608 (Massaponax Church Road). Follow CR 608 to US 1. Turn right on US 1 and get in the left lane. Turn on to CR 607, which goes all the way to Guinea Station and the small office where Jackson died. The route covers about 24 miles.

Fredericksburg

Fredericksburg is located in northeast Virginia off I-95 and VA 3, which is the road to the Chancellorsville battle site. Moss Neck, Jackson's headquarters, is about 11 miles south of Fredericksburg on US 17; the house itself is not visible from any public road. The former site of Belvoir—the home of Thomas Yerby, where Jackson had his famous profile photograph taken just weeks before his death—is near an elementary school close to the intersection of CR 635 and CR 608 just southeast of the city; the grave of the little girl who captivated Jackson is located there in a family cemetery that is not open to the public. The line Jackson held at Fredericksburg is on Lee Drive, just west of the intersection of US 1 Business and VA 3. The Confederate Cemetery—where Jackson's trusted civil engineer, Captain James Keith Boswell, is buried—is located downtown at William and Washington Streets.

In late November and early December 1862, the Union army under General Ambrose Burnside launched a new campaign to capture Richmond by heading overland and passing through Fredericksburg on the Rappahannock River. At first, the Federals moved so quickly that Lee almost failed to get in front of them at Fredericksburg. But because of a bureaucratic foul-up in Washington, Union pontoon boats necessary to bridge the Rappahannock were not delivered on schedule. By the time the boats were on hand, Lee was digging in on the south bank of the river.

Now that Burnside had lost the element of surprise, some of his generals suggested he abandon the idea of attacking, since Lee was in a perfect defensive position, on high ground above a river the Federals would have to cross before they could even start climbing toward him. But Burnside, anxious to prove himself to Lincoln, would not back down. He wanted to attack.

Robert E. Lee gave Stonewall Jackson a tough assignment: defend the south bank of the Rappahannock. While Longstreet's men would defend the high ridge on the left called Marye's Heights, which gave the defenders a clear field of fire down to the town, Jackson would defend the right flank. That part of the battlefield was much flatter, offering the Federals a better chance to attack the Confederates.

On December 13, Jackson met with Lee and Longstreet on Lee Hill, now preserved by the National Park Service on Lee Drive just west of the intersection of VA 3 and US 1 Business. Jackson was dressed in the new uniform J. E. B. Stuart had tailor-made for him back in October. Everyone was so used to seeing Jackson in his old, faded, blue V.M.I. coat that they did double-takes on seeing him in a new, fine, gray coat trimmed with gold braid.

As the generals looked to the north at the massing Federals, Longstreet asked Jackson if he was afraid of the Yankees he could see. Jackson answered, "Wait until they come a little nearer, and they shall either scare me or I shall scare them."

With that, Jackson returned to his headquarters, located just past the end of Lee Drive at Hamilton's Crossing, not far from where Lee had his headquarters on the railroad line. It was either at his tent headquarters at that point or earlier in the day that Jackson had a confrontation with his black servant, Jim Lewis. Jackson had called for Little Sorrel to be saddled. When Lewis showed up with another horse, Jackson demanded Little Sorrel. Lewis refused, saying Little Sorrel had been ridden hard for several days and deserved a rest. Lewis won the argument, and Jackson rode another horse.

When the battle was launched at about 10 o'clock that morning, Jackson faced 60,000 Federals. Unsure of his orders, the Union commander, General William Franklin, never threw in all of his troops. Had Franklin launched a major attack, he might have overwhelmed Jackson's line. As it was, Jackson's cannons, which had been hidden from view during a Federal cannonade, waited until the Federals were at close range before they opened up.

Later in the afternoon, some Federals swept into a gap in the Southern line and briefly breached the Confederate defenses. Jackson soon pushed back, and the Federal attack on his side of the line failed. In that attack, South Carolina general Maxcy Gregg was shot near the spine. Gregg had been an enemy of Jackson's ever since Jackson had arrested his regimental colonels for allowing their men to burn some fence rails to cook their rations.

That night, Jackson's conscience began to bother him as he thought about the mortally wounded Gregg. He decided to visit Gregg to settle their past differences. He rode to the Yerby House. Sitting on Gregg's bed, he said he knew that the general would soon die and that he wanted to apologize for any differences the two had in the past. "Turn your thoughts to God and to the world for which you go," Jackson said. Gregg thanked Jackson and grasped his hand. Gregg,

Jackson's line at Fredericksburg at the spot where General Maxcy Gregg fell mortally wounded

a leading politician who had helped take South Carolina out of the Union, died shortly afterward.

Within a few days, in response to a rumor that the Federals were crossing the Rappahannock below Fredericksburg, Jackson shifted his headquarters south of town to Moss Neck, a fine brick home owned by the Corbin family, one of the wealthiest families in the region before the war. Now, the home was beginning to show signs of wear, as Federal raiders had hit it several times.

Jackson refused to use the main house, though it was offered. Instead, he reluctantly accepted a small office building in front of the main house. On December 21, he hosted a dinner for top officers, who kidded Jackson about the fine accommodations and food that he had at his headquarters. They told him he should get out in the field and learn how real soldiers had to live—which, of course, was almost always the Jackson way. Jackson was embarrassed by all the teasing.

Jackson operated out of the house for three months, which was the longest time he occupied a headquarters. During that period, he sometimes saw six-year-old Jane Corbin, daughter of the owner of the house. For some reason, the little girl took to Jackson. It may have been that, in her presence, he dropped the gruff, grizzled, angry nature that he seemed to have with adults. For hours at a time, she would cut out paper dolls on the floor of Jackson's office while he attended to reports. Jackson, worried about the health of his own baby daughter, Julia, fell in love with Jane. On March 16, 1863, Jackson prepared to move out for the spring offensive. He stopped by to see Jane one last time. He was told she had scarlet fever but was recovering. The next morning, an aide brought Jackson shocking news. Little Jane had died the previous night, as had two little cousins. Jackson, the general who had ordered thousands of men to certain death without flinching, broke down sobbing. He then fell to his knees

Historical marker near Moss Neck, Jackson's headquarters in the winter of 1862–63. The house is not visible from the highway.

to ask God to receive Jane. It was only the second time Jackson's aides reported that he openly cried; the first had come upon hearing of the death of a favored elderly slave back in Lexington. Little Jane was buried in the Yerby family cemetery behind Belvoir.

Jackson enjoyed a visit with Anna and baby Julia at Belvoir on April 20, 1863. It was the first time he had seen the baby, who had been born five months earlier. On April 23, Julia was baptized in the parlor of the home. Oddly, Jackson and Anna gave the baby the middle name of Laura in honor of his Unionist sister, who had cut Jackson out of her life when he threw his lot with the Confederacy. Anna wrote Laura about the honor, but Laura did not respond.

Within a few days, Jackson sat for his second photograph of the war. Taken in the Yerby parlor, the photograph shows him facing right and wearing the fancy coat Stuart had bought for him. Mrs. Jackson preferred the almost-smiling, full-face photograph taken in November 1862 in Winchester to the stern-looking shot taken here. Jackson had his image taken only a few times during his life.

Jackson's trench line at Fredericksburg

On April 28, after visiting with his family for eight days, Jackson got word that Union general Joseph Hooker was moving to Lee's left, attempting to cross the Rappahannock River and move against the Army of Northern Virginia. Jackson packed Anna and Julia up and sent them to a train car to return south. They would see each other again in less than two weeks, but it would be the final time.

Before you leave Fredericksburg, pay a visit to the grave of Captain James Keith Boswell, located downtown in the Confederate Cemetery. Once you enter the cemetery, head toward the Confederate statue. Walk to the right and find the military burial ground. At the end of the line of graves, near the remains of General Daniel Ruggles, is the grave of Boswell, who was reburied here after first being laid to rest in the Lacy family cemetery west of Chancellorsville, where Stonewall's arm now lies.

Boswell, a civil engineer, found the roads and bridges that transported Jackson's army. Major Jed Hotchkiss made the maps from Boswell's information. Together, the two of them were the real secrets behind Jackson's ability to move his "foot cavalry" as fast as he did.

Boswell was riding with Jackson on his scouting mission on the night of May 2, 1863, when they were fired upon by a Confederate regiment that had no idea a scouting party was returning its way.

Boswell was killed instantly by two bullets to the chest. His friend Hotchkiss found his body the next morning lying where he had fallen from his horse. Hotchkiss wrapped his friend in a blanket and buried him in the Lacy family cemetery after a chaplain read a service.

Guinea Station, where Jackson died

Guinea Station

The plantation business office where Jackson died is known as the Stonewall Jackson Shrine. This National Park Service site is located south of Fredericksburg about five miles from Exit 118 off I-95. The house, inside and outside, looks exactly as it did in 1863. The room includes the bed in which Jackson died. The same clock that recorded the hour of his passing still sits on the mantel. Call 540-373-6122 for information and hours.

Following his wounding at Chancellorsville, Jackson arrived at Fairfield, the Chandler plantation, on May 4, 1863. It was the same railway stop where he had picked up his wife and baby daughter just 10 days earlier. The first thought was to put him inside the plantation house, but Chaplain Beverly Tucker Lacy decided that the house was too noisy, so he chose a small, whitewashed office building on the grounds as Jackson's care center.

When Jackson's ambulance arrived, the general told Mr. Chandler, "I am sorry that I cannot shake hands with you, but one arm is gone and my right hand is wounded."

Jackson's surgeon, Dr. Hunter Holmes McGuire, gave strict orders that no one other than himself, two aides (James Power Smith and Joseph Morrison), Chaplain Lacy, and Jim Lewis (Jackson's black servant) be allowed into the building. Morrison soon left. He rushed to Richmond to bring his sister—Jackson's wife, Anna—to see the general.

For two days, Jackson seemed to be doing as well as could be expected. The amputation of arms and legs was routine during the Civil War and even the Mexican War. The wounded frequently survived and even returned to the field. Jackson himself had one-legged Dick Ewell as one of his corps commanders. Ewell had suffered a shattered kneecap in August 1862 at the Battle of Groveton.

But on Thursday, May 7, Jackson woke with pain in his side. When McGuire listened to his chest, he heard the sounds of pneumonia. Doctors knew how to cut off arms. They did not know how to treat a patient whose lungs were filling with fluid. McGuire summoned other doctors to see if they could think of anything he was not already doing.

That afternoon, Anna, baby Julia, and Aunt Hetty—one of Jackson's slaves, who was acting as nurse to Julia—arrived at Fairfield. As soon as Anna saw her husband, she knew he would not survive. Jackson was pale and weak. He was not the man she had seen just a few days earlier.

On Friday and Saturday, Jackson grew weaker. Anna asked McGuire outright if Jackson would die, and he said yes. They both told Jackson that he would not survive. On Saturday afternoon,

Jackson asked to see his chaplain. But instead of requesting prayers for himself, he urged the chaplain to do what he could to promote the observance of the Sabbath in the army. The Sabbath had always been important to Jackson. He never wrote a letter that he thought would be in transit on Sunday. He even lobbied the Confederate Congress once to defeat a bill that called for mail to travel on Sunday to speed service. Ironically, no matter how hard he tried to control matters, many of his battles took place on Sunday.

When Sunday, May 10, 1863, dawned, it was obvious to everyone attending the general that he would not live the day. Anna told him so, and he asked the doctor to confirm it. When McGuire agreed, Jackson seemed to accept it. Anna then confirmed that he wanted to be buried in Lexington. Soon, five-month-old Julia was brought in to see her father. He played with her and talked to her.

Later, after his aide, Major Sandie Pendleton, told Jackson the army was praying for him, the general thanked him and said, "I always wanted to die on a Sunday."

In his last minutes, Jackson seemed to return to the battlefield, calling out the names of A. P. Hill and Pendleton. Then his eyes opened wide. He looked at the ceiling and seemed to sink back into the bed in relaxation. He said one final sentence: "Let us cross over the river and rest in the shade of the trees."

The bed where Jackson died at Guinea Station

Fredericks Hall

This hamlet is located on CR 618 just west of its intersection with CR 609 about 50 miles northwest of Richmond. There is little left here from Jackson's day.

Fredericks Hall appears to be about the same size today as it was in 1862. When Jackson arrived at the train stop here on June 22, 1862, he was determined to keep secret Lee's plan for him to move south toward Richmond. He spent a few hours sleeping in a local house, then jumped on a borrowed horse before dawn to head to his meeting with Lee. Jackson was so paranoid about being discovered that he tried to disguise his identity by carrying a pass written for an unnamed colonel. Since Jackson had not been in Richmond for more than a year and had not had his photograph taken, the ruse actually worked.

Jackson's secretive nature and his fatigue began to cause mistakes well before the battle plans for the defense of Richmond were even discussed. He trusted an aide, Major Robert Dabney, to act as his second-in-command. He instructed Dabney to go back and get his 18,500 men ready to move to Richmond. Jackson should have given precise instructions to one of his division commanders. Instead, he told a civilian minister who had no real concept of what it took to move an army. On top of that, Jackson gave his final instructions to Dabney on a Sunday. Dabney respected the Sabbath and did no real work on getting the army into motion until the next day.

Slash Church, on the line of march to the Seven Days' Battles

Ashland /Slash Church/Peak's Turnout

The town of Ashland is about 16 miles north of Richmond at the junction of US 1 and VA 54. Slash Church lies southeast of Ashland. From the historical marker for Jackson's march on US 1 in Ashland, turn east on CR 657 (Ashcake Road). Drive about four miles, turn left on Mount Herman Road, and go 0.3 mile to the church. Peak's Turnout is a tiny hamlet two miles from Slash Church at the intersection of Colefield Drive and Peaks Road. It lies about a mile west of US 301.

The exact route Jackson took from Fredericks Hall to Dabbs House in Richmond and back again before the Seven Days' Battles in June 1862 is not known. But it is known that he and his army passed through Ashland on June 25.

Slash Church was one of Jackson's march objectives. He was supposed to reach it on the first day's march toward Richmond, but the slow pace caused him to miss his mark by at least six miles. On the first critical marching day, Jackson was already behind.

Jackson was supposed to get started at two-thirty the next morning, but it was eight o'clock before the army got on the road. The men marched two miles beyond Slash Church to Peak's Turnout, another tiny hamlet along the railroad, which still looks much the same as it did in 1862. It was just past Peak's Turnout that the column split into two parts, Ewell heading down what is now US 301 and Jackson crossing US 301 and heading down what is now CR 651 (Georgetown Road).

Richmond

I-95 and I-64 are the major access routes to the city. The Museum of the Confederacy, the White House of the Confederacy, the Governor's Mansion, and the State Capitol are downtown. The Dabbs House is at the eastern edge of downtown on Nine Mile Road, which may be reached via Exit 193B off I-64.

Jackson's association with Richmond was limited to making a few brief visits while passing through on the way somewhere else.

The Museum of the Confederacy, located at 12th and Clay Streets, has some Jackson items, among them the forage cap he liked to pull low over his eyes. A more poignant artifact is the map book that engineer Keith Boswell was carrying in his breast pocket when he was riding with Jackson on the night of May 2, 1863. Boswell was killed by two bullets to the chest in the same volley that wounded Jackson in the arms. The map book shows the path one bullet took to Boswell's heart.

Next door is the White House of the Confederacy, which Jackson visited with Robert E. Lee after the Seven Days' Battles to dis-

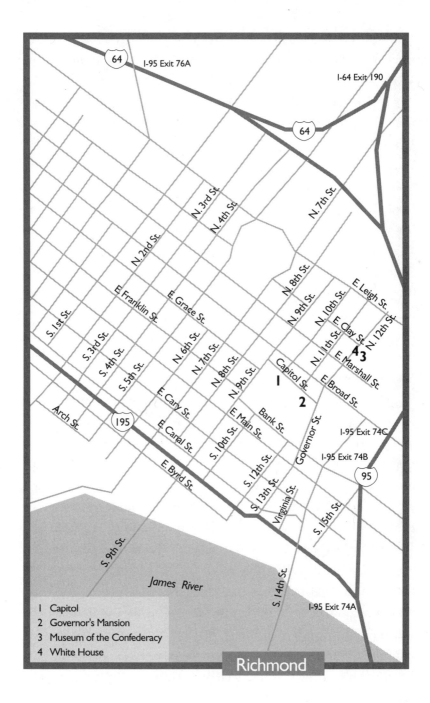

1 Capitol
2 Governor's Mansion
3 Museum of the Confederacy
4 White House

Richmond

cuss with President Jefferson Davis the upcoming campaign against General John Pope. For information on both the museum and the White House, call 804-649-1861.

Two blocks south of the museum is the Governor's Mansion, located on the edge of Capitol Square at Grace and 12th Streets. Jackson's body was embalmed here. It lay in state at the Governor's Mansion for one day, May 11, 1863. Covering the coffin was the Stainless Banner, the second national flag of the Confederacy. The Confederate battle flag was in the upper corner, and the rest of the flag was white. It was the first time the new flag had ever been used. The Governor's Mansion is closed to the public.

On May 12, Jackson's body lay in state in the old Senate Chamber of the nearby State Capitol. This was the same historic room where Lee had been welcomed as the general of Virginia's forces. According to estimates, more than 20,000 mourners passed through the State Capitol to see Jackson's body. The old Senate Chamber is open to visitors.

The most significant Jackson site in Richmond is the Dabbs House, located on the left side of Nine Mile Road less than a half-mile north of Exit 193 off I-64. Now the Henrico County Police Department headquarters, it has been restored to its wartime appearance. The Dabbs House was where Jackson conferred with Robert E. Lee and several other generals on the upcoming campaign to move Union general George McClellan from in front of Richmond. The campaign would come to be called the Seven Days' Battles.

Jackson reached the Dabbs House on the afternoon of June 23, 1862, having ridden all day from Fredericks Hall, 40 miles away. When he arrived, he was virtually reeling in the saddle from the accumulated exhaustion of the Shenandoah Valley Campaign in May and June and from sleeplessness over the past several days as he prepared for his secret trip to Richmond. He was leaning on a fence when the other generals arrived for the war council. All were surprised to see him, for they assumed—as did the Federals—that Jackson was still in the Shenandoah Valley.

This may have been the first time Lee and Jackson ever met in person. Certainly, it was the first time they spent any amount of time together. The two had exchanged letters, orders, and reports, but circumstances had never put them together to fight. Now, they were embarking on a campaign to save Richmond from McClellan.

The other generals at the meeting were Daniel Harvey Hill, Jackson's brother-in-law; James Longstreet; and Ambrose Powell Hill, an enemy of Jackson's from the day the two first saw each other at West Point as new cadets. D. H. Hill would later serve well with Jackson. A. P. Hill would serve unhappily under Jackson.

Of all the generals in the room, Jackson had done the most fighting and had been the most successful. Lee, in fact, had failed in his two previous attempts at conducting campaigns in western Virginia. Though he was commander of the Army of Northern Virginia, Lee had not actually been in a battle since the Mexican War. Even then, he had been only an engineering lieutenant, rather than a commander of men.

As Lee laid out his plan to hit McClellan's exposed right flank by secretly shifting most of his existing forces, plus using Jackson's men coming in from the Shenandoah Valley, Jackson was so exhausted that he barely seemed to pay attention. When he was asked how soon he could get his men into place, he had to be prompted to give a date. The date and time settled upon were very short—June 26 at three o'clock in the afternoon. It was currently June 23 at probably five in the afternoon or later. Jackson had therefore agreed to ride back to Fredericks Hall, pick up his 18,500 troops—who he assumed would be waiting for him—and march them into line ready for battle in just three days. Why Jackson or some other general did not insist to Lee that the battle be put off for one or even several days to allow Jackson and his men to rest has never been determined. Likely, Lee was worried that McClellan would realize his right flank was in danger and would pull it back. Whatever the reason, pushing a fatigued Jackson would prove to be a mistake.

Walnut Grove Church/Old Cold Harbor/ Grapevine Bridge/White Oak Swamp/ Malvern Hill

The sites associated with the Seven Days' Battles are located a few miles east of Richmond. For information, call Richmond National Battlefield Park at 804-226-1981.

Walnut Grove Church is at the intersection of CR 615 (Walnut Grove Church Road) and VA 156. From the church, drive 1.7 miles on CR 615, then turn right on Colts Neck Road. After a short distance, turn left on CR 635 (Sandy Valley Road). Drive 0.4 mile, then turn right on CR 633 (Beulah Church Road). Go 1.4 miles to where CR 633 runs into VA 156 to reach Old Cold Harbor. From this point, you can follow the National Park Service signs to Grapevine Bridge, White Oak Swamp, and Malvern Hill.

Lee and Jackson met at Walnut Grove Church on the morning of June 27, 1862, to discuss final tactics for what would come to be known as the Seven Days' Battles. The Battle of Beaver Dam Creek had already been fought on June 26 a short distance west of this location, when A. P. Hill had tired of waiting for Jackson and had

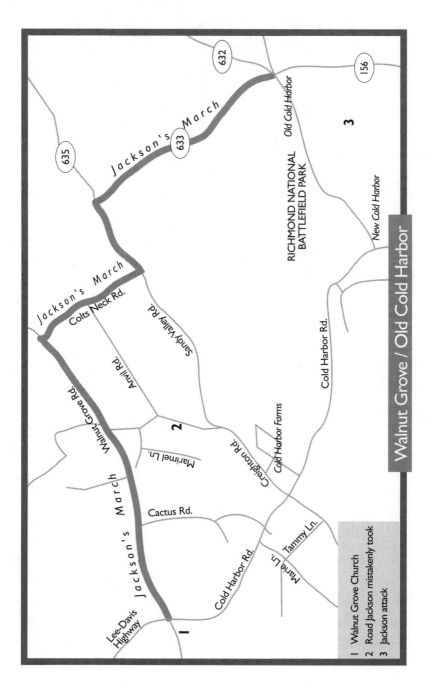

Walnut Grove / Old Cold Harbor

632

156

635

633

Jackson's March

Old Cold Harbor

3

RICHMOND NATIONAL
BATTLEFIELD PARK

New Cold Harbor

Jackson's March

Colts Neck Rd.

Sandy Valley Rd.

Anvil Rd.

Cold Harbor Rd.

Walnut Grove Rd.

Cold Harbor Farms

2

Marimel Ln.

Creighton Rd.

Jackson's March

Cactus Rd.

Tammy Ln.

Marie Ln.

Cold Harbor Rd.

Lee-Davis
Highway

1

1 Walnut Grove Church
2 Road Jackson mistakenly took
3 Jackson attack

Virginia
165

Walnut Grove Church, where Lee and Jackson met during the Seven Days' Campaign

attacked on his own. Both the Confederates and the Federals were then moving toward Gaines Mill, about two miles southwest of the church.

It was after this meeting that Jackson made a major mistake because he was unfamiliar with the territory and did not have the services of his mapmaker, Jed Hotchkiss, who had been left behind to draw more maps of the Shenandoah Valley. Lee ordered Jackson to move to the Federal right at Cold Harbor. What Jackson did not know was that there was a New Cold Harbor and an Old Cold Harbor, the latter located a short distance farther away.

Jackson began marching east on Walnut Grove Church Road. He asked a local guide to lead him to Cold Harbor, but he did not tell the guide what he wanted to do other than get his men there. The guide turned right down what is now Creighton Road about 1.1 miles from Walnut Grove Church. The entire force arrived near

Gaines Mill, which was too far to the right of where Jackson needed to be if he was to turn the Federal right. It was then that Jackson learned about the two Cold Harbors, and only then did he tell the guide exactly what he wanted to do. The angry guide blamed Jackson for the mistake, then had Jackson turn the army around and head back to Walnut Grove Church Road and from there to Old Cold Harbor, Jackson's true destination.

Old Cold Harbor was on the right of the Federals. Jackson was supposed to attack diagonally across what is now the intersection of VA 156 and CR 633, heading in a southwesterly direction, but only the front of his 18,500-man force was ready. Jackson sent Major John Harman, his quartermaster, back to bring up two divisions immediately. He gave Harman, a civilian before the war, a long, complicated verbal order, most of which Harman did not begin

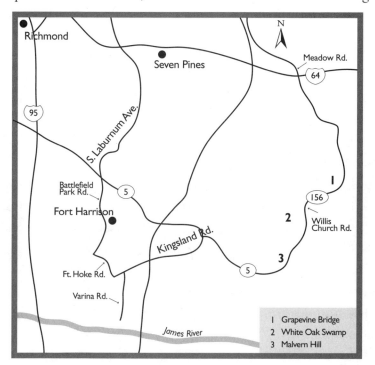

to understand. Harman rode back up Beulah Church Road, Colts Neck Road, and Walnut Grove Church Road looking for the commanders to whom he was to give the orders he did not understand. Those division commanders did not understand Harman's garbled orders. But instead of riding to find Jackson to clarify what he wanted, they did nothing—another mistake caused by Jackson's fatigue and his trust of someone who didn't know what he wanted.

Lee and Jackson met somewhere near Old Cold Harbor. Lee said, perhaps sarcastically, "General, I am glad to see you. I had hoped to be with you before!"

Several hours later, the Federals were defeated at Gaines Mill, but it was mostly men from Longstreet's division who did the heavy fighting. Though he helped the effort, Jackson was late due to going down the wrong road and did not deliver a crushing blow on the Federal right.

That evening, Jackson rode forward down what is now VA 156 to see what lay ahead for the third day of fighting. Somewhere west of Old Cold Harbor, he ran right into a tiny knot of Federals. The surprised Jackson ordered them to surrender to his aides, which they did.

Jackson's duty on June 28 seemed simple enough. He was to rebuild the Grapevine Bridge over the Chickahominy River, then move his troops over it in support of Longstreet, who was chasing the Federals into White Oak Swamp. Jackson later got a dispatch from Lee. He interpreted it to mean that he should protect the bridge once he finished rebuilding it. In fact, Lee wanted Jackson to support an attack by General John B. Magruder, but the order was so poorly written by a Lee staff member that Jackson stayed at the bridge while Magruder's men attacked alone at Savage Station, barely two miles away.

Follow the National Park Service signs for about 3.7 miles, watch-

The creek that creates White Oak Swamp Jackson's cannons shelled the far bank.

ing on the right for Portugee Road. Turn here, drive a short distance, then turn left on Red Coach Lane, which curves back around to Portugee Road. Here is the artillery position from which Jackson shelled the Federals on the other side of White Oak Swamp on June 30. The Federals initially ran from the bombardment, but they quickly rallied. Jackson risked his life by being one of the first Confederates on the other side of the creek. An artillery shell landed near him, but he was unharmed. Jackson spent most of the day dueling with the Federal artillery along the road, rather than looking for another place to cross. Longstreet later complained that his men were cut up in the fighting at Frayser's Farm while Jackson lounged on the other side of a tiny creek and a passable swamp.

Return to the National Park Service tour route and cross the bridge, the destroyed wooden version of which was used by Jackson. The hill on the left on the far side of the creek was one of the Federal artillery positions that vexed Jackson.

On July 1, Jackson crossed White Oak Swamp. The Federals who had contested it the day before were gone. Jackson seemed more alert now. Perhaps he had finally gotten a good night's sleep.

Follow the National Park Service tour signs for about four miles,

Federal cannons looking down Malvern Hill

then slow to view the cleared field on the left. This was likely the general area where Jackson tried to unlimber his cannons to fire on Malvern Hill, located about 0.7 mile ahead. The better-equipped Federals had longer-range cannons and very good gunners. They were able to smash most of Jackson's cannons before they even got rounds off.

Continue to Malvern Hill. Park your car and walk down to the row of Federal cannons. Jackson's position was in the distant tree line to the right in front of the cannons. These representative cannons were backed by 100 more on this hill. They were deadly accurate, something that Jackson refused to acknowledge. Instead of recognizing the peril his cannons were in, he ordered the gunners to do battle. Few were able to fire more than a round or two before they were destroyed by the Federals. Jackson then ordered D. H. Hill's infantry into a frontal assault. The cannons ripped into Hill's men such that Hill later commented, "That was not war. It was murder."

That night, Jackson went to bed near the knoll where his artil-

Field just northeast of Malvern Hill where Jackson tried to set up his cannons. Most were destroyed before firing a round.

lery had been destroyed. He slept so soundly that his staff could not wake him, even though they shouted in his ear and shook him.

The next day, July 2, he was up early ordering his men to clear the bodies from Malvern Hill. When asked why, he replied that he was planning to attack on that ground shortly and that he did not want his men stepping on the bodies of their dead comrades. Jackson was ready to fight.

That afternoon, Jackson met President Jefferson Davis for only the second time, the first having been their brief encounter at First Manassas. Lee made his headquarters at the Poindexter House, located northeast of Malvern Hill; the home no longer stands. Lee was meeting with his generals there when President Davis arrived unexpectedly. When Davis was introduced to Jackson, the two men stared at each other. Jackson held a grudge against Davis for overriding his orders and forcing the evacuation of Romney back in January. Davis knew that Jackson did not care for him. They did not shake hands.

Over the next couple of days, Lee and Jackson evaluated the Federal position. When they determined that it was strong, they mutually called off any further attack. Malvern Hill ended the Seven Days' Battles. Jackson had done poorly, but Lee and his fellow generals should never have placed such unrealistic demands on him and his men.

Maryland

1 White's Ford
2 Frederick
3 Boonsboro
4 Sharpsburg
5 Dam Number Five

IN THE FOOTSTEPS OF STONEWALL JACKSON
172

White's Ford

This is the spot where Jackson's army landed after crossing the Potomac on its way to Sharpsburg in September 1862. You can reach it if you're willing to take a walk. Drive two miles north from Beallsville on MD 28. Turn left on Martinsburg Road and drive another two miles, past a large power plant. Look on the right for a sign for Dickerson Park. Park your vehicle in the park and walk to the C & O Canal. Walk a half-mile south to Marker 39.5.

White's Ford, just north of Mason Island in the middle of the Potomac, was a familiar, busy spot during the war. Confederates and then Federals crossed the river here. During the Sharpsburg Campaign, most of Lee's army, under the command of Longstreet and Jackson, crossed here on the afternoon of September 5, 1862.

Many Southern soldiers—thousands of them—balked at the idea of invading the North. They had joined the war to defend their homes against a Union invasion, not to invade the North. In their eyes, two wrongs did not make a right, even if two beloved generals like Jackson and Lee were commanding them. Estimates are that Lee's army numbered about 55,000 in Virginia. When it crossed into Maryland, it may have numbered as low as 45,000. It was a lack of discipline Lee and Jackson could not control. Rather than detach still more men to arrest those who refused to cross the river, Lee simply crossed without them. Many of the men waited patiently on the Virginia side of the river and rejoined the army after the Battle of Sharpsburg.

Popular tradition says that, while crossing the knee-deep river, Jackson's men broke into "Maryland, My Maryland," a song of Southern sympathy that described the day early in the war when Union soldiers had shot into a crowd of Confederate supporters in Baltimore. Some historians think the vocal performance never happened, as tired soldiers were not likely to start belting out state songs on a hot day.

What definitely never happened was that Marylanders felt inspired to join Lee's army. The invasion of Maryland failed to generate a groundswell of recruiting in the state.

A major traffic jam occurred at White's Ford when 40,000 men and the wagons supporting them tried to cross the river. The soldiers scrambled up the slight bluff on the Maryland side, but the mules pulling the wagons decided they would just as soon stand awhile in the cool river. Jackson called on his quartermaster, Major John Harman, to get the wagon train moving. Harman employed a tactic that had always worked when untangling other such jams—he yelled profanity at both mules and wagon drivers alike. Jackson, the Presbyterian who never swore, listened without comment. He then thanked the major for getting the army across the river.

The Confederates arriving in Maryland were a rough-looking lot after almost four months of continuous fighting. One person wrote, "I have never seen a mass of such filthy, strong-smelling men." Another in Frederick wrote of "dirty, lank, ugly specimens of humanity, with shocks of hair sticking through holes in their hats, and thick dust on their dirty faces." But that same writer also recognized that the Confederates could fight: "These men had coped and countered successfully, and driven back again and again and again our splendid legions with their fine discipline."

Frederick

Frederick is located at the junction of I-70, US 340, and US 15 about 30 miles west of Baltimore and about 10 miles from the Potomac River. The historic downtown area has one Stonewall Jackson site, the Evangelical Reformed Church (formerly the German Reformed Church) at 15 West Church Street, just one block west of the visitor center. This was where Jackson attended church on the Sunday before the Battle of Sharpsburg. Located on MD 355 (Urbana Turnpike) about three miles south of downtown and one mile north of Monocracy National Battlefield is a historical marker for Best Grove, the headquarters of Lee, Jackson, and Longstreet.

On September 5, 1862, Jackson finally achieved what he had wanted for more than a year and a half: an invasion of the North. On the same day he crossed the Potomac at White's Ford, admiring (or maybe conspiring) Marylanders presented him with a horse. It was a large, gray mare that really did not suit his preference for smaller, thinner horses like Little Sorrel. But Little Sorrel happened to be missing at that time, either taken as a prank or stolen. Since

Jackson needed an extra horse, he accepted the gift horse without looking her in the mouth—and apparently without riding her to see if she suited him. That was a mistake that could have cost him his life.

On the morning on September 6, Jackson mounted the horse at his overnight camp at Three Springs, located about 12 miles south of Frederick at a site that is unmarked today. When the mare wouldn't move, Jackson touched her with his spurs. Instead of walking forward, the horse reared and fell backward, taking Jackson to the ground with her. He was so stunned that he did not move for a half-hour. His surgeon suggested that he ride in an ambulance for several days. Jackson asked his brother-in-law, General D. H. Hill, to take over field command of the corps until he recovered.

If anyone was looking for signs of good luck, the opening of the Maryland campaign did not offer them. Just a week earlier at Second Manassas, Robert E. Lee had fallen while trying to catch the reins of Traveller, who had been spooked by false cries that Federal cavalry was attacking. Lee sprained one 56-year-old wrist and broke the other. Both of his hands were in wooden splints. Now, two generals were confined to rough-riding ambulances. On top of that, the other top general, James Longstreet, was unable to wear boots because of a blister on his heel. Longstreet's men must have wondered why their beloved general was walking and riding around in open-heeled carpet slippers.

Jackson rode in his ambulance to Best Grove, the farm of the Best family, where he made his camp near Lee and Longstreet. It was unusual for the top three generals to camp next to each other, rather than closer to their individual commands. This may indicate how closely they thought they needed to coordinate their movements in their full-scale assault on the North. It was from Best Grove that Lee issued a written plea for Marylanders to join his army and fight for the Southern cause. The lack of response was embarrassing, proving once and for all that Maryland, while having Southern sympathies, was solidly a Union state.

Curious Marylanders flocked to the camp for a sight of the two legends, Lee and Jackson. One story says that Jackson was walking from his tent to Lee's when he was ambushed by two young women who had ridden out from town just to meet him. Jackson had no problem fighting Federal forces many times the size of his own, but he had no idea how to combat two teenage groupies. Once they left, satisfied after seeing their hero, he went back to his tent and did not emerge until darkness had driven all the townspeople to their homes.

On the evening of September 7, Jackson proved yet again what a stickler he was for regulations. He had missed Sunday-morning church service, so he wanted to catch a service in town that evening. He invited his aides to accompany him. Just before leaving, he asked them if they had obtained passes to get them through the lines.

"No. You are the commanding general. You don't need a pass," one answered.

Jackson told the aide that any soldier trying to enter Frederick needed a pass.

The amused aide wrote out a pass to "Maj. Gen. T. J. Jackson" to attend church and to return that night, then signed it, "By Command of Major Genl. Jackson."

Satisfied that the commanding general had approved the pass, the commanding general then went to church.

It was the first time Jackson had seen Frederick. Later, from his tent, he wrote wife Anna that "the town appears to be a charming place, neat and beautiful. The ladies and gentlemen were sitting in front of the doors and all looked some comfortable, and I may say elegant, according to my ideas, and their enjoyment looked so genuine, that my heart was in sympathy with the surroundings. If such scenes could only surround me in Lexington, how my heart would, under a smiling Providence, rejoice!"

Jackson and his aides—including Henry Kyd Douglas, who had written the pass—went to the German Reformed Church because the local Presbyterian church did not have an evening service. Jackson sat in a rear pew and promptly fell asleep, as he admitted in a letter to his wife. He tried to make the claim that he fell asleep because he could not hear the minister from the rear pew. The truth was that the deeply religious Jackson always fell asleep in whatever church he attended, whether in peacetime or wartime. "[Jackson's] head sunk upon his breast, his cap dropped from his hands to the floor, the prayers of the congregation did not disturb him and only the choir and the deep-toned organ awakened him," Douglas wrote.

It was in Lee's tent at Best Grove on the evening of September 9 that the final strategy for the Maryland invasion took shape. Lee, Longstreet, and Jackson discussed the problem of what to do about Harpers Ferry and its garrison of 12,000 Federals just 20 miles away. Lee had expected the Federal command in Washington to order the town abandoned when it learned he was moving into Maryland. Instead, Washington, perhaps anticipating that Harpers Ferry would present Lee a major problem, ordered the garrison to stay in place.

That Harpers Ferry garrison had to be neutralized, lest it move against Lee's supply line back in Virginia or attack the wagon trains that would be following the infantry. Longstreet voted to move the entire army against the garrison, on the theory that it didn't make sense to divide the army in enemy territory. Jackson argued for Lee's suggested option, which was to split the army. According to that plan, Jackson's corps would head toward Harpers Ferry and split into three parts to surround the town. Lee theorized that the Union commander, General George McClellan, would be too slow and careful in chasing the Confederates and would never even know that half

Best Grove, south of Frederick, Maryland, served as a headquarters for Lee and Jackson.

of the Southern army had headed toward Harpers Ferry. Having fought McClellan just three months earlier during the Peninsula Campaign east of Richmond, Lee remembered that McClellan was always hesitant about using his army.

Jackson displayed his rarely seen sense of humor in pushing for the attack on Harpers Ferry. He told Lee that he had some "friends in the [Shenandoah] Valley" he had been "neglecting," referring to the Federals he had fought four months earlier.

Lee shot back that those particular friends would not be delighted to see him again.

Longstreet was irritated that neither Lee nor Jackson gave weight to his opinion that dividing the already small army was dangerous, but he understood he was outvoted and didn't argue.

It was then that Lee started drawing up the most complicated order of the entire war, Special Orders 191. The order spelled out Jackson's mission to Harpers Ferry, Longstreet's mission to remain with Lee, and D. H. Hill's mission to guard the passes up South Mountain east of Sharpsburg. Jackson's half of the army would split into three parts and would be 20 miles away from Lee's half, which would split into quarters. On top of that, the Potomac River would be between the halves. If it started raining and the river began to rise, each half would be on its own with no expectation of support from the other.

Copies of Special Orders 191 were prepared for all division commanders. The order was considered so secret that Longstreet ate his once he memorized it. Jackson made a copy for D. H. Hill, whose division would split off from Jackson's corps. Jackson was apparently unaware that Lee was also having his staff prepare a copy for Hill. There was now an extra copy of the order that might not be immediately missed.

Within a couple of days, the Army of Northern Virginia departed Best Grove and the Union army moved into the same campground. On September 13, at a site across MD 355 and a little closer to the river, a Union soldier looked down on the ground and saw a yellow envelope. Inside were three cigars and two pieces of paper. Those papers were a copy of Special Orders 191. Recognizing their importance, the soldier went directly to his commander. The papers were passed up the chain until they reached McClellan's tent. McClellan ran around his headquarters tent waving the order and shouting, "With this I can whip Bobby Lee!" Indeed, he made such a show that a Southern sympathizer rushed after Lee to inform him that his plan had fallen into Union hands.

There are many unanswered questions about the lost order.

Who lost it? For decades, detractors who never liked the sour, independent D. H. Hill claimed he was the culprit, but that story apparently was false. Hill said he received only one copy of the order, and that it was the one from Jackson. That copy exists today in the Hill family's papers.

If not Hill, who was responsible? Evidence is circumstantial at best, but some historians point the finger at Henry Kyd Douglas. After Lee's aide copied the order for the division commanders, he gave a copy to an unidentified "Virginia staff officer" hanging around the headquarters camp, who volunteered to take it to Hill. It is known that Douglas was a star-struck young officer who enjoyed being near the seat of power and playing the role of aide to Jackson. As a member of Jackson's staff, he would have known where Hill's headquarters were located. And finally, Douglas smoked cigars. Douglas certainly never admitted losing the order in his writings, but he fits the description.

Why would Lee's aide give a secret order to someone he didn't know by name? If he did know that man's identity, why wouldn't he lay blame at the feet of the person who actually lost the order? If the officer was a Jackson staffer who knew Jackson already had the order and had already copied it, why would he accept another copy? Why didn't Douglas—or whoever the officer was—report that the order was lost? How could it have gotten lost so close to where the officer received it? If the courier got to Hill and discovered that the envelope had fallen out of his pocket, why didn't he retrace his steps to find it? Why wasn't the envelope noticed by one of the thousands of Confederates camped right there in the field? How could something as valuable to a common soldier as cigars have remained unnoticed for three days until discovered by Federals?

The mystery of Special Orders 191 will likely never be solved.

Visitors should note that there is a museum in Frederick devoted to Barbara Fritchie. But don't be fooled by John Greenleaf Whittier's famous poem claiming that Fritchie defied Jackson by flying a Union flag from her window, and that Jackson admired her bravery. Jackson never rode down her street, never heard of her, and never saw her.

Boonsboro

Jackson had a close call at Boonsboro, which lies about 15 miles northwest of Frederick at the junction of US 40 Alternate (called the National Road during the war) and MD 34. He spent the night of September 10, 1862, at the home of John Murdock. That house is located at 6524 West Main Street (US 40 Alternate) about a mile east of town. The Boonsborough Museum, located at 113 North Main Street, has some Jackson-related artifacts. Call 301-432-6969 for hours and information.

When Jackson left Frederick on the morning of September 10, he made it a point to ask several citizens what roads to take to reach Pennsylvania. If the civilians had known anything about Jackson, they would have realized they were being set up to throw off any pursuers. Jackson never even told his own commanders where they were going, so he certainly wouldn't have asked civilians for directions he really needed.

Jackson's true destination was Harpers Ferry. Because he wanted to make sure that Martinsburg (northwest of Harpers Ferry) was subdued and because he also wanted to give the impression that he was heading north, Jackson chose a roundabout route that covered nearly 70 miles. His men climbed over two mountains, including South Mountain, which his brother-in-law, D. H. Hill, would later defend with several regiments of North Carolinians once McClellan started his pursuit.

Jackson was on the outskirts of Boonsboro walking toward town when a Federal cavalry patrol chasing two of his aides came rushing toward him. Jackson escaped, but he likely began to suspect that his force had been discovered.

Jackson stayed at the house of John Murdock, a Southern sympathizer in an area of Unionist feeling. It is a private residence today. That night at the Murdock home, Jackson released General A. P. Hill from the arrest he had been under since the two had argued over the way Hill marched his men east of Leesburg, Virginia. The charges were not dropped but merely delayed until Jackson could call a proper court-martial. One of Jackson's consistencies was that once he grew angry at an officer, he remained angry.

From Boonsboro, the Confederates crossed south over the Potomac near Williamsport and swung through Martinsburg. Jackson had been an unknown colonel when he was stationed north of the town a year and a half earlier, but he now found himself a famous general who had to fight off admirers. The Confederates then moved to Bolivar Heights west of Harpers Ferry, where Jackson waited for the other two segments of his force to close in from the north and east.

Sharpsburg

This small town is located near the Potomac at the junction of MD 65 and MD 34 about four miles northeast of Shepherdstown, West Virginia. Its compact business district is not much bigger than it was in 1862, when George McClellan and more than 80,000 Union troops clashed with Robert E. Lee, who fought most of the battle with just 25,000 men. Jackson met with Lee at the Grove House, Lee's first headquarters, which still stands as a private dwelling on the town square downtown. Antietam National Park is just northeast of town. A small fee is charged. Call 301-432-5124 for information on the battlefield.

Of all the major Civil War battlefields, Sharpsburg (called Antietam by the North, after the creek that runs through the battleground) is the easiest to understand because it was fought in three distinct locations at three times of the day. Jackson's portion of the battlefield was on the left, behind, and north of the small, white Dunker Church just northwest of the visitor center.

Looking at Sharpsburg's position on a map is chilling from a Southern perspective and encouraging from a Northern perspective. The only reason Lee chose to fight here once a copy of his invasion plan for Maryland was discovered in an open field near Frederick was because his army's far-flung four parts could reunite using the four roads that intersected in the farming town. Lee's original plan was to strike deep into Pennsylvania, and perhaps to march on Harrisburg to capture that capital. But once McClellan saw the lost copy of Special Orders 191, which laid out the disposition of Lee's army, Lee had to stop in his tracks and gather the fingers of his army into one central core. The best place to do that was Sharpsburg, since roads led to it from Shepherdstown and South Mountain, the outer edges of the army's location.

But Sharpsburg is just a few miles from the Potomac River—the wide, sometimes-shallow, sometimes-deep Potomac. It took hours for Lee's men and wagons to secretly cross the river. It would take many more hours for them to retreat back across it if they were being chased by a Union army three times their size. One of the almost unbreakable rules of warfare even today is to not fight a battle with your back to a river, because an overpowering enemy can push you. The Potomac could have swallowed Lee's entire army, and the war would have been essentially over in the Eastern Theater.

While some historians believe he may have been able to pull the main body of his army back across the Potomac, Lee felt he had no choice but to fight at Sharpsburg. He could not leave D. H. Hill's division at South Mountain or Jackson's divisions at Harpers Ferry to be cut off and cut up. He had to bring the entire army together. He also believed that his men were spoiling for a fight on Northern soil as payback for the deprivations that were being inflicted on Southern civilians. Coming off victories in the Seven Days' Battles, Cedar Mountain, and Second Manassas—all in Virginia—Lee believed his men, though heavily outnumbered, could withstand any onslaught.

Perhaps the greatest factor in Lee's favor was his opponent, George McClellan, a general Lee had defeated in June during the Seven Days' Battles. McClellan had left that battlefield fully convinced that Lee's army was twice the size of the Army of the Potomac, rather than half its size. His opinion had not changed, though he actually had three times Lee's manpower now, since thousands of Confederate troops had refused to invade the North. McClellan had proven to be slow to move and quick to frighten. Lee would count on those traits at Sharpsburg.

Jackson and his 6,000 troops arrived at Sharpsburg after an all-night march from Harpers Ferry about midmorning on September 16, 1862. Jackson, who had not slept in more than a day since beginning the attack on Harpers Ferry, met Lee at the Grove House, where he got his order to defend the Confederate left. It was at the Grove House that Lee told all his generals that they would stand and fight at Sharpsburg. Lee later moved his headquarters a half-mile farther west to a marked field on the north side of what is now MD 34. The new site allowed him to remain out of sight of Union gunners.

Jackson rode to the German Baptist Brethren meeting house, a plain, whitewashed, square structure on the Confederate left. The members of this church were much like Quakers in their beliefs in

The Grove House, where Jackson met Lee in downtown Sharpsburg

not making war and not making a showy display of their faith. Their practice of fully dipping members of the congregation into the river for baptism gave them their nickname: Dunkers. The "Dunker Church" did not have a steeple, something that was foreign to the devout Presbyterian general, who was used to seeing church buildings that pointed to God. Jackson did not use the church as a headquarters. He set up a tent on Hauser's Ridge, located northwest of the church behind the simply named West Woods. Apparently realizing that people would seek him out if he stayed in his headquarters tent, he lay down against some tree roots to grab his first sleep in two days. He did not rest long before the duty of preparing for the coming fight consumed him.

At first light, a wave of Federals under the command of General Joseph Hooker came sweeping out of Miller's Corn Field, located to the northeast. Their objective was to capture the high ground they could see around and behind the Dunker Church—Jackson's headquarters. Among the Federals heading toward Jackson was General William Henry French, Jackson's senior officer at Fort Meade, Florida. It was a squabble with French that had convinced Jackson to

The Dunker meeting house at Sharpsburg, the focus of the Federal attack on the West Woods

leave the United States Army in 1851 and accept his professorship at Virginia Military Institute.

For several hours, the battle flowed back and forth, Jackson's men taking terrible fire. At one point, his line came close to collapsing until it was bolstered by reenforcements. Finally, after smashing an attack by a Federal division that was hit by Confederate and accidental Union fire from three sides, Jackson regained control of the West Woods. Near the end of the battle, an unexploded shell landed near Jackson, but he did not flinch. Instead, he contemplated leaving the safety of the woods and attacking. His flabbergasted subordinate generals and colonels were stunned that he would consider such a thing after losing almost half his men. Jackson finally thought better of the idea after seeing the Union cannons he would have to face. After four hours of fighting, the Battle of Sharpsburg shifted to the right toward a sunken farm road defended by Jackson's brother-in-law, D. H. Hill.

That night, Jackson made his camp south of Lee's tent on what is now MD 34. The next morning, he saw that the Union army was still in place. Though he thought an attack might be possible, he eventually concurred with Lee that the army should retreat back across

Boteler's Ford below Shepherdstown.

Jackson's men acted as a rear guard as the army crossed the river back into Virginia that night. John Harman, Jackson's quartermaster, cursed, slapped the backsides of mules, and did whatever else was necessary to untangle the great traffic jam of men and wagons, just as he had done a few days earlier at White's Ford below Frederick, when the army had been invading Maryland. Boteler's Ford can be accessed from the Maryland side by leaving your car at the C & O Canal parking lot, located on the left of MD 34 just before the Potomac, then walking east one mile on the towpath to Marker 71.39. It was also here that some Federals crossed in pursuit of Jackson and were virtually wiped out on the opposite shore.

Visitors may also want to view Ferry Hill Place, located on the right side of MD 34 before the C & O Canal. Now the National Park Service headquarters for the canal, this was the boyhood home of Henry Kyd Douglas, Jackson's youngest staff aide.

Dam Number Five

This dam spans the Potomac River between West Virginia and Maryland. From Williamsport, Maryland, on the north side of the river, drive about five miles north on MD 68. Turn left on MD 56, which has a sign pointing toward Fort Frederick State Park. At the first stop sign, turn left on Dam Number Five Road. After about three miles, the road dead-ends at Dam Number Five, located on the historic C & O Canal.

There is something poetic about a stone wall defeating Stonewall (who had gotten his famous nickname five months earlier). It happened at Dam Number Five.

Though the Potomac River was filled with rocks that made boat traffic difficult in many places, the Chesapeake & Ohio Canal—which ran from Washington, D.C., to Cumberland, Maryland, a distance of more than 150 miles—enabled the Federals to move supplies up and down the river. Jackson and the Confederate high command in Richmond reasoned that if Dam Number Five above Williamsport were destroyed, the C & O Canal would likely be left without sufficient water to float barges. That would make it more difficult for the Union to ship supplies west.

On December 7, 1861, Jackson ordered a regiment under the command of an old Lexington friend, Major Frank "Bull" Paxton, to destroy the dam. In Jackson's mind, an order was something to be carried out. It did not matter how difficult the assignment was, how many Federals might be encountered along the way, or what nature might bring. An order was an order. When Paxton returned a few days later with the unhappy news that he had barely dented the dam because of Federals shooting from the Maryland shore, Jackson was livid. He was not going to let a stone wall defended by a handful of Federals get the better of him.

Dam Number Five on the Potomac

On December 14, Jackson himself set out from Martinsburg with his full brigade. The Confederates began the second attack on December 17. To his irritation, Jackson could do little better with five regiments than Paxton had done with one. Whenever his men went into the water to try to place gunpowder to blow big holes in the dam, they were fired upon from the opposite shore, less than 300 yards away.

Jackson may not have tried to blow down the dam using cannons. Or perhaps the Confederates fired shells and cannonballs that failed to damage the dam, since it was entirely underwater. In the end, it was men in the water using crowbars who finally knocked a hole in the structure. The lake behind the dam began to drain downriver. Satisfied, Jackson and his men withdrew to Martinsburg.

The minor damage Jackson's men caused was easily repaired. Once the Confederates left, the Federals simply rowed over to the Virginia shore and repaired the damage. The lake re-formed within a few days. Jackson apparently chose to ignore news that Dam Number Five was back in action. He had wrecked it once. That was enough for him. He returned to Winchester to begin the campaign to capture and occupy Romney before hard winter came.

One of the famous stories about Jackson got its start during his four cold nights at Dam Number Five. His doctor, Hunter Holmes McGuire, insisted that Jackson take a drink of whiskey to warm his insides. Jackson did so. When McGuire asked him if the whiskey tasted good, Jackson replied, "I like it. That is why I don't drink it." Perhaps the stories of his father, stepfather, and uncles being drinkers had stuck with Jackson and made him uneasy about the possibility that he could also be susceptible. The general did his best to keep alcohol out of the hands of his men, though he did understand its value as a calming medicine when administered by doctors.

It is interesting to note that early in the war, Jackson strongly advocated ignoring Maryland's neutrality and attacking Union troops wherever he found them. Yet he did all his fighting at Dam Number Five from the Virginia side of the river. Reports indicate that Jackson's force was much larger than the Union contingent defending the dam, but he apparently made no effort to send his men across the river to the Maryland side to root out the enemy that was making his mission so difficult. Though Jackson likely could have dispatched or captured the entire Maryland force, he chose to strictly follow the orders he had been given to stay on his side of the river. It was this Jackson trait—following orders—that began to attract the attention of Lee, who had been embarrassed that fall when two generals who were supposed to report to him virtually ignored his requests and orders. Within six months of his effort to destroy Dam Number Five, Jackson would be reporting directly to Lee—and obeying everything he was told to do.

The site of Cottage Home, where Jackson married Anna Morrison

NORTH CAROLINA

Cottage Home

The house where both Thomas J. Jackson and Daniel Harvey Hill married two of the Morrison sisters (at different times) no longer stands. It was accidentally burned down in the early 1900s when one of the sisters came for a visit. The site is identified by a historical marker just in front of a Duke Energy electric power plant. From I-77 north of Charlotte, take NC 73 West, then turn south on NC 16. Drive 2.3 miles, turn right on CR 1511 (Old NC 273), and go another 2.3 miles to the marker on the right. The site of the home is still surrounded by a grove of trees planted by the Reverend Robert H. Morrison, Jackson's father-in-law. To visit the graves of Jackson's in-laws, continue four miles on CR 1511 to the intersection with CR 1360, where you'll find Machpelah Church and its cemetery.

Something about the daughters of Presbyterian ministers appealed to Jackson. He married two of them—one, Ellie, in Lexington in 1852 and the other, Anna, here at Cottage Home in 1857. Ellie died in childbirth. Anna survived Jackson by many years and became a celebrity in her own right.

The Morrison sisters had something that attracted military men. One married Daniel Harvey Hill, who became a Confederate general. Another married Rufus Barringer, who became a Confederate general after his wife's death. Another married one of the most famous generals of all time. She was Mary Anna Morrison, called Anna.

While it was not unusual for women of the 1850s to marry men with whom they had not been intimate, the courtship of Anna Morrison and Professor Thomas J. Jackson may have set the standard for lack of close contact. Jackson met Anna and her sisters when they went to Lexington to visit D. H. Hill and his wife, their sister. At that time, Jackson was close to being engaged to Elinor Junkin, daughter of the president of Washington College. When he visited the Hills' home, Jackson enjoyed the company of the Morrison girls, all of whom were witty conversationalists, an art Jackson was practicing.

When Ellie died in childbirth, Jackson grieved for a while, then began to think of someone else to marry. He remembered Anna Morrison, whom he had not seen for four years. He wrote her a letter recalling that single visit to Lexington. Anna's sisters, who were aware that Jackson was now a widower, predicted that he would come to visit her.

In 1856, the Hills were living in Davidson, North Carolina, where D. H. Hill was a mathematics professor at Davidson College, founded by the Reverend R. H. Morrison. Just before Christmas, Hill happened to ask one of the Morrison servants if Anna had any suitors. The servant mentioned that a man with very large feet was visiting

The graves of Dr. and Mrs. R. H. Morrison, Jackson's in-laws

The grave of Captain Joseph Morrison, brother-in-law of Jackson, who was at the general's deathbed

her as they spoke. Hill instantly recognized his old friend Jackson from that description.

It is unknown whether Jackson actually proposed to Anna during that visit to Cottage Home. What does seem clear is that both of them began to think of themselves as being in a long-distance romance once Jackson went back to Lexington.

The marriage was set for July 16, 1857. Jackson arrived several days in advance and stayed with the Hills in Davidson. Their house no longer stands. As has been the case with countless weddings through time, things did not go particularly well for the couple. The bride's dress arrived at Cottage Home only two hours before the ceremony. Jackson could not make his fancy collar stand up. He apparently was married in his V.M.I. uniform—likely the same coat he would wear when he went off to war in four years.

It appears Jackson never visited Cottage Home again. Anna returned here after his death. Little Sorrel, Jackson's war horse, roamed the property for a while.

Those few days Jackson spent in North Carolina in 1856 and 1857 brought him the happiest times of his life.

The remains of Jackson's in-laws, the Reverend and Mrs. R. H. Morrison, and of his brother-in-law and military aide, Joseph Morrison, lie along the wall in the cemetery at Machpelah Church. Joseph Morrison was with Jackson during most of his final days and was almost killed in the same volley that wounded Jackson.

Wilmington

Wilmington is on the North Carolina coast at the eastern terminus of I-40. US 17, US 421, and US 74/76 also give access to the city. Oakdale Cemetery is located at the end of 15th Street, six blocks north of the intersection of Market and 15th.

Stonewall Jackson never visited Wilmington, but there is a significant site associated with him here.

John Decatur Barry must have been a natural leader. Just 22 when he joined the 18th North Carolina as a private, he was soon elected captain of that regiment. After Sharpsburg, he was promoted to major at age 23. He climbed the ranks until he was nominated for general in 1864—quite an accomplishment for a 25-year-old. However, he was wounded in the hand before the promotion came through, so he remained a colonel. Forced to retire from the field because of unspecified broken health, he returned home to Wilmington. He died in 1867 at the tender age of 27 and was buried in Oakdale Cemetery.

Normally, Barry would not attract special attention, as his war career mirrored that of many other men. But he did something of considerable note. On May 2, 1863, Major Barry ordered the volley from the 18th North Carolina that tore into Stonewall Jackson and his staff as they returned from a scouting mission in front of the lines at Chancellorsville.

It was not Barry's fault. Jackson didn't tell him or any other regimental commander that he would be riding in front of their lines. As Jackson and the 18 other members of the scouting party returned from the direction of the Federals, they made no effort to identify themselves to the nervous front-line Confederate regiments. Indeed, they sounded very much like a Union cavalry attack as they wheeled around in the darkness.

A single shot rang out from the Confederate lines. Then a ragged volley came from the Seventh North Carolina, posted on the right side of the road.

Joe Morrison, Jackson's brother-in-law, shouted, "Cease firing! You are firing into your own men!"

Major Barry shouted a reply directed at the 18th North Carolina, posted on the left: "Who gave that order? It's a lie! Pour it into them, men!" Just a few minutes earlier, Barry's men had been approached by a Federal patrol that had tried the same tactic, shouting that they were friends. Barry was not about to be fooled this time.

A full volley from dozens of muskets blazed out of the darkness from the 18th North Carolina. Minie balls from three Enfield rifled muskets found their way into Jackson's right hand and left arm and shoulder. He died eight days later.

Barry does not seem to have been blamed for ordering the volley that wounded his commanding officer. In fact, he was promoted to colonel after Chancellorsville, based on his performance. His obituary does not even mention the Jackson shooting. It praises his career and laments his early passing.

If you are visiting Oakdale Cemetery on a weekday, stop at the office for a map, as this is a large cemetery with many crisscrossing, unmarked roads. Upon entering the cemetery, bear to the left, then turn right on the first paved road. Follow this road until it makes a slow, sweeping turn to the left. After passing the third paved road to the right, stop your vehicle and walk down the grass road that leads past a tombstone for the Fonvielle family. On the right just past this tombstone is the grave of Colonel John Barry.

Barry seems to be buried alone. No other family member is nearby. His small tombstone has an inscription that echoes a statement Napoleon Bonaparte made about one of his generals: "I met him a pygmy and lost him a giant." It is fitting for a man who joined the army as a private and very nearly made general.

Barry's lonely little plot seems sad, almost as if no one wanted to be buried beside the man who mistakenly ordered that fatal volley.

The site of Fort Meade, Jackson's last posting in
the United States Army

Fort Meade

This small town is located at the intersection of US 17 and US 98 about 50 miles east of Tampa. The site of the second fort here—the location and construction of which led to Jackson's resignation from the United States Army—is now a city park and playground bordered by Orange Avenue, Cleveland Avenue, First Street, and Third Street. It lies a few blocks east of the intersection of US 17 and US 98. A nearby historical marker incorrectly states that Lieutenant George Meade, the man for whom the fort was named, went on to become "commander of United States forces" during the Civil War. Meade actually commanded the Army of the Potomac, one of several Union armies fighting in the war.

In the 1850s, Fort Meade was not a place where an ambitious

officer wanted to be stationed. It was not really a fort at all, but rather a collection of buildings on the banks of the Peace River. The Peace was not much of a river either, as it was barely 30 yards wide. Fort Meade was simply an outpost along a military road established 20 years earlier as part of the United States government's attempt to suppress the Seminole Indians.

The fort's value was questionable, since there were hardly any Seminoles left to suppress. Beginning in 1818, the Seminoles fought the United States Army in two fitful wars that the army failed to win decisively. After that, most of the Indians were relocated. Those who escaped the clutches of the army melted into the woods and the swamps of the Everglades, 100 miles south of the fort. The fort was surrounded by wilderness that held little but swamps, quicksand, rattlesnakes, alligators, and mosquitoes carrying malaria and yellow fever. There was no major settlement of white people nearby. The only "civilization" was the 60 or so soldiers right there on the post, all of whom were bored to death.

Captain William French, the new commander, had served with Jackson on court-martial duty in New York State. He decided there was one thing he could do to keep his men busy: rebuild the fort on a higher ridge about a half-mile west of the river. That would prevent it from being washed away in the event of heavy rains. It would also give the fort a better look at the terrain in the unlikely event it was ever attacked by Indians.

Jackson, reassigned from Fort Hamilton in Brooklyn, New York, was a busy man at Fort Meade. He assumed the role of quartermaster and acted as engineer in the construction of the new fort's buildings.

In January 1851, Jackson went on his first scouting mission in Florida, taking a patrol to Lake Tohopekaliga, about 40 miles northeast of Fort Meade (near where Disney World stands today). Jackson and his 14-man patrol marched 90 miles in six days and did not see a single Seminole. The best Jackson could do was report that he had found two wooden poles that he thought might have been used by Indians to cook their game. An incredulous French let Jackson rest a few days, then sent him out again. On the second patrol, Jackson again found no Indians.

At that point, French decided to lead a patrol himself, which came as an insult to Jackson and the rest of the fort. French was effectively saying that he did not believe the patrols had done a good job. If they couldn't find any Indians, he would.

Jackson wrote his sister in March 1851, "I like scouting very much, as it gives me relish for everything, but it would be still more desirable if I could have an occasional encounter with Indian parties."

He considered Fort Meade a giant roadblock in his military career. Within two months of arriving, he put in two applications through military channels. One was for a leave of absence that would allow him to travel to Europe. The other was for a transfer to another post. The seemingly contradictory applications may have been Jackson's way of covering his bases. If he got transferred, he likely would not have followed through with the leave of absence. If he got the leave of absence, he would hope that his slot at Fort Meade would be filled by another officer who would still be there when he returned to duty. Either option might bring a better shot at a more active post—perhaps someplace in Texas, where Indians were shooting at settlers and soldiers alike.

In February 1851, Jackson got a letter in the mail that changed his life. It was from Francis H. Smith, superintendent of Virginia Military Institute in Lexington, a place Jackson had never even visited. The letter asked if Jackson would like to be considered for a position as professor of natural and experimental philosophy. Though

Smith did not tell Jackson, his name had been put into consideration by Washington College professor Daniel Harvey Hill, a Mexican War acquaintance and Jackson's future brother-in-law.

The same day, Jackson wrote a reply to Smith. It read in part, "Though strong ties bind me to the army, yet I can not consent to decline so flattering an offer. Please present my name to the Board and accept my thanks for your kindness."

Jackson did not get his hopes up about the new position, but his immediate reply suggests that he was looking for any way out of Fort Meade.

In late March 1851, Jackson and French started down a course from which there was no return. They began to clash over who had final say in the construction of the new fort. Jackson thought he was in charge, since he was acting quartermaster. French, as camp commander, justly felt he was in charge of where the fort should be located.

Jackson started the ball rolling downhill when he wrote a letter to Colonel Thomas Childs complaining that French was not following regulations that supposedly proved Jackson should be in charge of building the new fort. Childs, stationed at Fort Myers, was the

Swampy area on the Peace River at the site of the original Fort Meade, Florida

overall commander of the forts in Florida. According to military protocol, Jackson's letter went first to French. French forwarded the letter after reading it, but he added his own comments that he had been supervising the construction of the fort all along, and that it made no sense for the camp commander to be less important than an acting camp quartermaster.

Jackson then escalated the disagreement by "cutting" French, an irritating military custom whereby he spoke to French only during official reporting duties but ignored his very existence at all other times. When Jackson passed French on the post, he did not even look up to recognize his presence.

They heard back from Colonel Childs in late March. Childs sided with French. Since French was the commanding officer of the post, it was Jackson's duty to act as quartermaster in any fashion French decided.

Jackson, always a man to hold a grudge, did not accept this outcome gracefully.

Within days of getting Childs's letter, French went off on his own scouting mission, since he did not trust the results of Jackson's two missions in search of Indians. Jackson was left in charge of the fort.

The day after French departed, Jackson wrote his sister that he was under consideration for a V.M.I. professorship and would take it if it was offered. Jackson was so angry that he was ready to leave the army.

The incident that finally ended Jackson's United States Army career started that April. Captain French was the only officer who had brought his wife to the wilds of central Florida. He also brought a dark-skinned servant girl, Julia. When Mrs. French became ill and French was seen occasionally walking with Julia, rumors began to float around the fort that French and the girl were having an affair.

On April 12, Jackson took it upon himself to question many of the fort's enlisted men about their knowledge of French and Julia. Those men had participated in spreading the rumors, but they did not like being put on the spot in an official investigation. One sergeant questioned by Jackson went right to French when he returned from his scouting mission and told him what his quartermaster was doing. French immediately placed Jackson under arrest and confined him to quarters. Jackson retaliated by writing a letter to headquarters saying that French was guilty of "conduct unbecoming an officer and a gentleman." He also claimed that French had placed him under arrest for conducting an investigation. He asked for a court of inquiry.

Over the next several days, French and Jackson traded written charges, Jackson going so far as to name dates when he believed French had relations with Julia. French countered that Julia had been in his employ for years and that he walked with her out of respect, since she was a woman on a remote military base. Both men demanded courts of inquiry. Those demands fell on deaf ears when a new department commander came on board. He was General David Twiggs, one of the longest-serving officers in the army and a man who was not about to start his new posting with a squabble between officers at a remote fort. He curtly informed French and Jackson that he was not about to do anything with either's charges.

In late April, Jackson received a second letter from V.M.I. He had been elected professor. He immediately sent back a letter accepting the position.

In May 1851, Jackson left Fort Meade forever. He never saw French face to face again, though the two men did square off against each other during the Seven Days' Battles.

PENNSYLVANIA

Carlisle Barracks

Carlisle Barracks is located near the intersection of US 11 and I-81 southwest of Harrisburg.

Little remains of the military base Jackson knew when he pulled court-martial duty here in 1848 and 1849. That is because his future friend J. E. B. Stuart burned the cavalry training base to the ground on his way to Gettysburg in 1863.

Still, Carlisle Barracks—an active military base and the home of the United States Army War College today—may hold some interest for Civil War historians, as it allows civilians to do research in its library.

New York City

In late 1848, Jackson was assigned to Fort Hamilton, now located under the west end of the Verrazano Narrows Bridge in Brooklyn on I-278. To reach the fort by subway from Manhattan, take the R train to the end of the line at 95th Street in Brooklyn and walk south toward the bridge. Upon reaching a small public park with a huge Civil War-era cannon—the largest ever cast—turn left to find the 100th Street entrance to Fort Hamilton. As this is a working military base, you will be expected to show photo identification and state your purpose, which is to visit the Harbor Defense Museum. Once inside the base, turn immediately right and walk one block to the museum. Admission is free. Call 718-630-4349 for details.

St. John's Episcopal Church, where Jackson was baptized as a Christian in 1849, is a few blocks away from the fort at Fort Hamilton Parkway and 99th Street. It is open most mornings at nine o'clock. The font used to baptize Jackson is on display in the back of the church.

Jackson brought his second bride, Anna, to see bustling

The only permanent military installation where both Stonewall Jackson and Robert E. Lee were assigned for duty is located in Brooklyn. Fort Hamilton went into service in 1831. Named after Secretary of the Treasury Alexander Hamilton, it is still an active military base. Only part of the fort's original casements remain. The remaining section has been converted into an officers' club, but the facility is open to the general public for lunch. The stone staircase inside originally went up to a tier of cannons guarding the entrance to New York Harbor. Jackson practiced firing those cannons into the water. One structure that can be visited is the caponier, a small, triangular fort just east of the main walls. The caponier was designed to force attacking troops to split on either side of it, at which time they could be fired upon from both the caponier and the main fort. The caponier now houses the Harbor Defense Museum.

Jackson arrived at the fort as an artillery officer in December 1848, two years after Lee had left it as an engineering officer. The two may have met briefly in Mexico during the war, but since Jackson was a brand-new West Point graduate, it is doubtful that they would have spent much time together, as there was an age difference of 17 years. It would be another 13 years before their paths crossed again.

As an artillery officer with nothing to shoot at, Jackson had good, light duty compared to Lee, who had come to the fort to fix leaks in its walls and roof. Jackson was often able to complete his reports early. When he could, he caught a boat across the river to Manhattan to visit bookstores and art galleries.

It was at Fort Hamilton that Jackson received his two brevet promotions, a confusing practice in those days of giving an officer honorary rank increases while his official rank remained the same. Jackson, officially a lieutenant in the United States Army, received brevet promotions to captain and then major based on his heroic actions at the Battle of Chapultepec, Mexico, where he had continued to fire his battery of cannons while under heavy attack. He used the brevet rank of major while teaching at Virginia Military Institute, though he was really a lieutenant when he resigned from the army in 1851.

It was also at Fort Hamilton that Jackson began to develop his reputation as an oddball, a tag that would follow him for the rest of his life because it fit. Though just 25 years old, Jackson thought

Fort Hamilton, New York, with Verrazano Narrows Bridge in background

himself sickly. He walked, did calisthenics, and lifted weights but never developed a muscular build, fluctuating between 155 and 166 pounds on a five-foot-eleven frame. While in his mid-20s, he began to have indigestion problems—or at least to think he had indigestion problems. With the help of Manhattan doctors who were apparently the forerunners of today's diet gurus, he developed his own eating regimen.

Once his fellow officers noticed that Jackson took fruit only before noon and that he ate only day-old bread, only the yolks of eggs, only one vegetable at meals, and only fresh meat, they began to look at him with new eyes. He was no longer the hero of the Battle of Chapultepec. He was now an officer who was becoming "shaky," to quote one man who wrote his family about Jackson.

Jackson's concern with food bordered on the ridiculous. He was invited to parties around the fort, as he was a young, eligible bachelor. Hostesses were often surprised to see him show up with his own food, since he did not expect that day-old bread would be served. Once, he shocked a hostess when he told her that he preferred to eat his food without pepper, as it made his left leg hurt.

On top of having a bad stomach, Jackson suffered from "weak eyes." Once, he claimed in a letter to his sister that he could not look out a window into the bright sunlight or even at a candle in a dark room without suffering pain. Yet he refused to investigate wearing glasses, claiming that his eyes would become dependent on them and grow even weaker.

It is unknown whether he developed his good-health notions on his own or learned them from medical quacks. When asked why he sometimes raised one arm above his head for no apparent reason, he answered that he was allowing the blood in it to drain back into his body, so he would not become unbalanced.

It was during his time at Fort Hamilton that Jackson became

interested in hydrotherapy, or water cures. "Taking the waters" encompassed drinking large quantities of fresh spring water—which supposedly contained valuable minerals—and bathing in cold, warm, or hot springs, no matter the season. Jackson became a habitual visitor to springs scattered all the way from Vermont to the far reaches of Virginia, a practice he kept up until the beginning of the war. He even captured a health spa early in the war and no doubt partook of its supposed curative powers.

Luckily for Jackson, the army realized that an artillery officer with nothing to shoot at could be put to work on other bases. During the two years he was officially stationed at Fort Hamilton, Jackson sometimes traveled for weeks at a time to other bases—such as Carlisle Barracks in Pennsylvania and Fort Ontario in New York—to serve court-martial duty. His practice was to research the locations of water-cure establishments and stop on the way to or from his court-martial proceedings.

The building at 47 Bond Street in the NoHo neighborhood in Manhattan, where Jackson visited a hydrotherapy doctor

Jackson also developed the spiritual side of his character at Fort Hamilton. Until that time, he had never been a particularly religious man, as might be expected of an orphan raised by an uncle who paid little attention to religion or ethics. While in Mexico, Jackson had investigated Catholicism, using the Spanish he learned at West Point to ask pointed questions of the local priests. It must have seemed strange to the priests that an American officer who had just helped conquer their country would have any interest in their religion.

One of Jackson's fellow officers at Fort Hamilton convinced him that it was logical that a man—particularly a soldier who could die violently at any moment during a war—should have a religion that would help him face his destiny. Jackson, always a man who respected logic, bought that argument. He began studying the common religions to see which one fit his character. Since he already knew something about Catholicism, and since the chaplain of Fort Hamilton was the Episcopal priest who headed Trinity Church in Manhattan, Jackson began learning about the Episcopal faith. On April 29, 1849, he was baptized at St. John's Episcopal Church, located just a few blocks from the fort. It was the same church where Robert E. Lee

Trinity Church on Wall Street

St. John's Episcopal Church,
where Jackson was baptized
in Brooklyn, New York

Baptismal font at St. John's
Episcopal Church

had been a vestryman. Though baptized in an Episcopal church, Jackson was careful not to declare himself an Episcopalian. He would finally choose to become a Presbyterian after lengthy discussions with a Presbyterian minister in Lexington.

There was something curious about Jackson's baptism. The priest who performed it wrote the name in the parish register as Thomas Jefferson Jackson. Jackson had adopted the middle initial *J.* at West Point to prevent his being confused with another cadet named Thomas Jackson. Historians have always assumed that the initial stood for Jonathan, after Jackson's father, though Jackson was never given a middle name by his parents. Could Jackson, who had begun reading history books to pass the time at Fort Hamilton, have adopted *Jefferson* in honor of Thomas Jefferson? Perhaps the priest mistakenly wrote it, but that seems unlikely, since the two had spent some time together studying the Episcopal faith. Perhaps it was a slip of the pen. Or perhaps the middle name shows an insight into Jackson's developing sense of self.

Jackson's court-martial duties away from Fort Hamilton occasionally took him to Fort Columbus (later renamed Fort Jay) on Governor's Island in New York Harbor just off Manhattan. The fort, built in the classic star shape to give converging fields of fire to the defenders inside, still survives on the 172-acre island, but access is restricted to the general public until the federal government and the governments of New York State and New York City figure out the island's future.

Manhattan attracted Jackson's attention as a place where, in his words, "everything is in motion, everything alive with animation." While stationed at Fort Hamilton, he often caught boat rides across the river to visit Manhattan art galleries and bookstores. His sister, excited that she had a brother in the center of fashionable society, asked him what the New York ladies were wearing. He told her in a letter than he did not even know the names of the parts of ladies' apparel.

Jackson also went to Manhattan to visit doctors and to sightsee on his honeymoons.

In 1851, he visited Dr. Roland Houghton, who lived and practiced at 47 Bond Street. They had met two years earlier. In fact, it was Houghton who introduced Jackson to hydrotherapy. While being treated by Houghton, Jackson met the doctor's father-in-law, Dr. Lowry Barney, who ran a clinic at Belleville, New York, near Lake Ontario. The clinic emphasized exercise and diet. Jackson went on to spend six weeks at Barney's clinic. Among the foods Barney suggested were buttermilk and cornbread, which became part of the bland diet Jackson adopted for the rest of his life. Whether doctors like Houghton and Barney were quacks or not, Jackson believed in them. More than two years after his stay at Barney's clinic, Jackson wrote a letter to the doctor saying, "I have derived so much benefit from your wholesome and wise instruction that gratitude to you will accompany me to the grave."

The honeymoon trips to Manhattan came in 1853 with Ellie, who would die in childbirth the next year, and in 1857 with Anna. Jackson and Anna climbed inside the spire of Trinity Church to see the skyline. They reported, "The view was indeed grand, embracing the whole city—graceful sparkling rivers, the bay and sound, studded with vessels at motion and at rest; and beautiful rural scenery stretching out as far as the eye could reach."

In the summer of 1858, Jackson and Anna made one final vacation visit to Manhattan. During that trip, Jackson made an appointment to see Dr. John Murray Carnochan, who removed part of his right tonsil. Anna sought the doctor's care several months later when she suffered an attack of facial paralysis, one of Carnochan's specialties. Later chief of surgery at New York Medical College, Carnochan became famous. His house and office stood on Lafayette Place just a few blocks from the office of Dr. Houghton. The homes in that area were eventually renumbered. No house on the correct side of the street today appears old enough to have been Dr. Carnochan's.

West Point

The United States Military Academy is located at West Point, on the west bank of the Hudson River about 40 miles north of New York City. The academy has a visitor center and a small museum. The grounds are open for touring, but the barracks and classrooms are closed to the public. For more information, call the visitor center at 845-938-2638 or the museum at 845-938-2703.

Thomas Jackson really did not belong at the United States Military Academy.

First of all, he did not win an appointment. Gibson Butcher, a friend from Weston, Virginia (now West Virginia), beat him in the qualifying tests and won the appointment. But after one day of military discipline at West Point, Butcher decided to reject the appointment and go home. When Jackson heard the news, he quickly gathered letters of recommendation and made his way to Washington, D.C., to tell his congressman, Samuel Lewis Hays, that he would take Butcher's place. The congressman, who did not know Butcher had even left West Point, agreed. He even walked Jackson down to the secretary of war's office to get the secretary to sign the official orders Jackson would need to present to the superintendent.

Second of all, Jackson was undereducated. His formal schooling had been hit or miss. It had been dependent on when there was a schoolteacher willing to come to the mountains of western Virginia. It had also fluctuated according to what chores around Jackson's Mill he had to complete. By comparison, most of the other cadets had spent years in what today would be considered high school or prep school. Some of them had actually left college in order to enter West Point. Jackson likely ranked among the lowest cadets in his existing knowledge of the subjects he would be expected to learn. On top of that, Butcher had used up the several months cadets normally spent studying for final entrance exams. Jackson was thus thrown immediately into the grind to make the grade. He started behind, and only by force of will and by virtue of help from other cadets was he able to overcome his academic limitations.

Third, Jackson had little experience dealing with people outside his own family and his mountain hometown. While many of his classmates came from the well-mannered wealthy class, Jackson had no knowledge of such things as manners and public speaking, which officers were expected to know. He had no idea how to make friends of strangers. When Jackson arrived at West Point, he was clad in homespun clothes, an old hat, and huge brogans. He looked more like a local farmer who had wandered on to campus than a future officer, much less a future general. Almost immediately, he was the butt of jokes and whispers about his appearance and serious nature. Among those who poked fun at the gawky cadet was a refined young man by the name of Ambrose Powell Hill. Jackson and A. P. Hill would dislike each other for the next 17 years, though Hill would prove an able fighter under Jackson.

Once Jackson got into West Point, the institution became the parents he never had. In one sense, the academy even gave Jackson a middle initial and maybe a middle name. Until he went to West Point, Jackson had always called himself Thomas or Tom. But in one letter to his sister while at West Point, he asked her to address her letters to Thomas J. Jackson to distinguish him from Thomas K. Jackson, another cadet. Most people assume that *J.* stands for Jonathan, his father's name, but Jackson himself never made it clear what the *J.* was supposed to mean. The priest in Brooklyn who baptized Jackson wrote his middle name as Jefferson. It has never been determined if that was a mistake or if Jackson told the priest his middle name was Jefferson.

Everything that Jackson employed in the rest of his life he learned at the academy—discipline, applying his talents to achieve an end, analyzing an enemy's strengths and weaknesses. It was at the academy that he started collecting his famous maxims of living, the sentences that expressed the goals he set for himself. The most famous ideal he developed is still closely associated with him: "You may be whatever you resolve to be."

In his first two years at West Point, Jackson struggled and likely avoided dismissal only with the help of a cadet named W. H. C. Whiting, another future Confederate general. Whiting took on Jackson as a personal project, tutoring him until he understood the complex subjects. Thanks to Whiting, Jackson finally got the hang of most of his subjects and improved his class standing each year. Several of his classmates, who finally grew to respect the odd young man, speculated that Cadet Jackson would have graduated at the head of his class had it been a five- or six-year program. The only subject at which Jackson utterly failed was drawing, which almost certainly precluded him from being assigned to the engineering corps, the preferred choice among highly rated cadets. He was also judged a poor horseman, though he had ridden racehorses as a child jockey. On the other hand, he was very good at geometry and mathematics, tools that came in handy after graduation when he was assigned to the artillery during the Mexican War.

Jackson's favorite spot at West Point was Fort Putnam, a stone fort built during the American Revolution, long before there was a United States Military Academy. During their free time, most cadets preferred resting or figuring out ways to get to Benny Havens, a nearby bar. But Jackson liked hiking up the mountainside to Fort Putnam, which gave him a commanding view of the parade ground and the barracks below. The fort is not always open today; check with the West Point Museum about hours. To visit the fort, take Stony Lonesome Road around the backside of Michie Stadium and turn on to Delafield Road.

Another spot familiar to Jackson was the parade ground, located in front of the barracks and the superintendent's house. The same parade ground is still used today. Another remnant from Jackson's day is the Old Cadet Chapel, built in 1837 and located in front of the West Point Cemetery.

It sounds odd, but the man who would become one of the best and most famous soldiers in American history did not believe he

Fort Putnam above the United States Military Academy

Fort Putnam looking down on the United States Military Academy. Jackson often visited the fort to think.

would make the military his career. Even before he graduated, Jackson wrote letters to his sister saying that he intended to stay in the army only long enough to fulfill the personal commitment he felt he owed the government for paying for his education. "I intend to remain in the army no longer than I can get rid of it with honor, and means to commence some professional business at home," he wrote her in 1843.

And what profession came to mind when Jackson considered civilian pursuits? His only experience with a paying civilian job had been a brief stint as a constable, a role in which he had been more of a process server than a sheriff's deputy or peacekeeper. In addition to serving legal papers on people, Jackson had experience watching his uncle Cummins sue his neighbors for infractions real and imagined. He had also noticed that lawyers seemed to get paid whether they won their lawsuits or not. As early as 1845, one year before he graduated from the academy, Jackson wrote to his sister that he was thinking of becoming a lawyer. He later changed his mind, even though an attorney offered to take him in and teach him to read law. Jackson told that lawyer that if another war came, he would likely be named a general, so he would stay in the army.

Niagara Falls

Niagara Falls is in the far northwest corner of New York State, north of Buffalo. It is accessible off I-190. Jackson spent both his honeymoons at the Cataract House, a famous hotel that burned down in 1945. The Comfort Inn-The Pointe now occupies the site. It is the closest hotel to the falls on the American side.

Behind the gruff exterior of Thomas J. Jackson was the heart of a lonely man who desperately wanted to share his life with a wife who would bear him children. He knew how to romance a woman: take her to Niagara Falls for their honeymoon.

Jackson and his first wife, Ellie, went to Niagara Falls in August 1853. They had an unexpected guest along—Ellie's sister Margaret, called "Maggie," who felt cheated out of her best friend when Jackson took her sister in marriage. If Jackson objected to having a third wheel along on a romantic trip, he kept it to himself.

Jackson was fascinated by the falls. He wrote his sister, "This of all natural curiosities is the most sublime and imposing which has ever come under my observation. When looking at this wonder of nature, I desired to be left to my own uninterrupted thoughts."

The visit came long before powered boat trips to the falls. It was while being rowed across the river below the falls that Jackson became exasperated with his new sister-in-law. Apparently, she had a panic attack as they approached the roaring water and began to stand up in the small boat. Jackson lunged for her before she could capsize it and pinned her in her seat. In a calm voice, he asked the boatman how long he had been rowing people on the river.

"Twelve years" came the reply.

Jackson then asked if he had ever lost anyone overboard.

"Nothing of the kind, sir," the man said.

Jackson then told his sister-in-law, "You hear what the boatman says; and unless you think you can take oars and row better than he does, sit still and trust him as I do."

Jackson, Ellie, and Maggie went from Niagara Falls to Montreal.

While starting married life with a hanger-on like Maggie must have been difficult for Jackson, he later came to respect—and maybe love—her. Ellie died in 1854 after delivering a stillborn son. She and Jackson had been married just 14 months. After Ellie's death, Jackson and Maggie became as close as the standards of the day allowed. Both were Presbyterians. Church law at that time dictated that a man could not marry the sister of his dead wife. The two respected that law but developed a friendship that survived until Jackson's death. Maggie went on to become a famed chronicler of life in the South during the War Between the States, writing as Margaret Junkin Preston.

Jackson returned to Niagara Falls in 1857 with his second wife, Anna. Interestingly, the registration book of the Cataract House shows that Jackson and Anna checked in just six days after a "Mr. A. Lincoln and family" of Springfield, Illinois, stayed there on a summer vacation. General Stonewall Jackson would be giving President Abraham Lincoln fits within five years of their near-encounter at the falls.

Fort Ontario

The town of Oswego is on the shore of Lake Ontario in upstate New York. It lies about 40 miles northwest of Syracuse at the end of NY 481. Fort Ontario is located at the mouth of the Oswego River on East Ninth Street in Oswego.

Jackson visited Fort Ontario in August 1850 for court-martial duty. He wrote his sister a letter that he was only a 12-hour ride from Niagara Falls and that he intended to visit the growing tourist attraction. He also told her that he wanted to visit an unnamed "water cure establishment" because "my health is so delicate as to render much regularity necessary."

Fort Ontario is now part of New York's system of state parks. Though it is preserved the way it was in 1867, some 17 years after Jackson was here, it likely looks much the way it did during his visit.

Plattsburgh Barracks

The town of Plattsburgh is in far northeastern New York State near the Canadian border. It is just off I-87. The now-closed military base is on US 9.

Jackson spent six weeks in the early summer of 1850 on court-martial duty at Plattsburgh Barracks. The army base eventually became a United States Air Force base, which was shut down in the mid-1990s. Many of those buildings remain, though there seems to be nothing left from Jackson's day beyond the "charming scenery" around Lake Champlain that he described to his sister and confidant, Laura.

Lieutenant Jackson's service at Plattsburgh was of little consequence except for the presence of another man assigned to court-martial duty—Captain William H. French. French and Jackson had known each other since the Mexican War but were more acquaintances than friends. Anyone wanting to rise in rank in the peacetime army knew he was always competing with others, so friendships were carefully guarded. If Jackson developed any hard feelings for French as his superior during his time at Plattsburgh, he kept them to himself or at least did not tell Laura.

Like Jackson, French was someone who read and followed the army manuals. It was an interpretation of army rules that would pit these two against each other in six months, after they were transferred to Fort Meade in central Florida. Jackson finally ended his feud with French in Florida by resigning from the United States Army.

Eleven years later, French faced Jackson on several Virginia battlefields. French never developed the reputation that Jackson, his former underling, did. In fact, French was blamed for not taking advantage of Lee during the Mine Run Campaign of November 1863 and was forced out of field service after reaching corps commander level.

MASSACHUSETTS

Northampton

Northampton lies along I-91 in west-central Massachusetts. It is about 20 miles north of Springfield. Several buildings and guesthouses from a water-cure establishment Jackson visited here are now part of the renowned Clarke School for the Deaf on Round Hill Road. Access to the campus is controlled. To arrange a visit, call the president's office at 413-584-3450.

In ill health in the summer of 1860, Jackson and Anna departed Lexington to take a water cure at Brattleboro, Vermont. Though that course of treatment proved a disappointment, Jackson was not about to give up on the idea of the curative powers of water. He and Anna simply moved 50 miles south to the renowned Round Hill Water Cure Retreat in downtown Northampton.

In the early 1840s, David Ruggles, a free black man active in the antislavery movement, came to Mill River, a town near Northampton, at the invitation of a benefactor. Almost blind and exhausted from his efforts at organizing the Underground Railroad, Ruggles claimed to be rejuvenated by undergoing the water-cure treatment practiced by Dr. Wesselhoeft of Brattleboro. Ruggles subsequently established his own water-cure establishment, which he promised would cure "headache, tendency of blood to the head, cold extremities, general and nervous debility, bronchitis," and about 20 other health problems. Wealthy people from all over the Northeast began to flock to this black "doctor," who had no education at all.

Success breeds competition. Two doctors in Northampton began their own water-cure establishment at Round Hill. Ironically, Ruggles, the man who started the local water-cure craze, died of unknown causes in 1849 at age 38. A young doctor, recognizing an established market when he saw one, bought Ruggles's property and renamed it Munde's Water Cure Establishment.

Round Hill, located several miles from Ruggles's original establishment, was a resort of 50 acres, most of it crisscrossed by walking paths, which were considered an essential part of the treatment. Running water was piped to the interconnected guesthouses and treatment centers. Round Hill also offered a broad range of exercise facilities, including bowling alleys.

Whatever the "doctors" in Northampton tried seemed to work for Jackson and Anna. Jackson, who had been plagued by fever, proclaimed himself cured. Anna, who had been almost unable to walk, was soon hiking five miles a day.

The Democratic Party broke into three pieces while the Jacksons were at Northampton that summer. It was a political disaster that seemed to guarantee that the Republicans, headed by Abraham Lincoln, would win the fall election. The South had been threatening to secede if that happened. The Jacksons felt that the other guests at Round Hill, most of them wealthy New Englanders, began to treat them differently as talk of war between North and South became more open. Anna wrote that her husband "heard and saw enough to awaken his fears that it might portend civil war; but he had no dispute with them who differed from him treating all politely and making some pleasant acquaintances."

Jackson had to leave Anna at Round Hill in August to prepare for the incoming fall class at V.M.I. She had been told by her doctor that it would be at least October before she was fully cured.

When Jackson left Northampton, it marked the end of his visits to the North until he arrived in Maryland in 1862 as an invading general.

VERMONT

Brattleboro

Brattleboro is in southern Vermont just off I-91. The brook that was once the site of a water-cure establishment still runs through the town.

Not even the threat of war could stop Thomas Jackson from the pursuit of a good water cure in the far Northern states.

In the spring of 1860, Jackson and Anna were both in ill health. Jackson believed he was suffering from a kidney ailment and thought it could be cured only by hydrotherapy. One clue to what was ailing him was that he said it was painful to ride in a carriage. Perhaps he had kidney stones. Perhaps all the mineral water he had been drinking as a health aid had instead contributed to his problem. Anna's ailments were more worrisome. According to Jackson, she could barely walk. And she sometimes suffered from facial paralysis.

As soon as the class of 1860 graduated from V.M.I., Jackson and Anna left Lexington for Vermont to try the Brattleboro Hydropathic Establishment of Dr. Robert Wesselhoeft. Wesselhoeft had "discovered" several springs that he claimed were healthful. The springs lay along Whetstone Brook in downtown Brattleboro.

Jackson and Anna were disappointed. After a stay of two weeks in the tiny town, during which they took the waters daily, nothing had changed for either of them.

The fire station at 103 Elliott Street alongside Whetstone Brook sits on the property where Dr. Wesselhoeft's establishment was once located.

Quebec City

Quebec City lies on the north bank of the St. Lawrence River about 120 miles northeast of Montreal. The Plains of Abraham—also called National Battlefield Park—is about a mile west of the St. Louis Gate in Old Quebec.

After leaving Niagara Falls in the late summer of 1853, the honeymooning threesome—Jackson; his wife, Ellie; and his sister-in-law, Maggie—arrived in Quebec City following a visit to Montreal. The hotel where they stayed and the sites they visited in Montreal are unknown.

It was in Montreal that Jackson and his new bride had their first spat. Jackson heard that a British Highland regiment was giving a drill in town and told the sisters he would be going to see it. Ellie and Maggie, the daughters of a Presbyterian pastor, were appalled. It was Sunday, and it shocked them that Jackson would go to a military demonstration instead of observing the Sabbath as a day of rest and reflection. Jackson refused to listen and attended the drill. That night, the sisters ganged up on him again and accused him of being less than Christian. Interestingly, Jackson later adopted their idea that Sundays should be kept holy. His most famous concession was that he would not mail a letter that would be in transit on a Sunday. Neither would he open a letter and read it on Sunday. Instead, he would wait until Monday. Contrary to his desire, circumstances during the war frequently had him fighting on Sundays.

When they reached Quebec City, where the British had won a major battle over the French in the French and Indian War of 1759, Jackson insisted on visiting the Plains of Abraham, still a Quebec City park. This was the site where British commander James Wolfe and his French counterpart, Montcalm, had done battle.

Maggie watched in surprise when Jackson doffed his cap as he approached a monument to Wolfe. She described the scene this way: "His clear blue eyes flashing, his thin, sensitive nostrils quivering with emotion, and his lips parting with a rush of excited utterance, as he turned his face towards the setting sun, swept his arm with a passionate movement around the plain and exclaimed, quoting Wolfe's dying words: 'I die content!' Then Jackson added with a trembling voice: 'To die as he died, who would not die content?' "

One wonders what it was about Wolfe that fascinated Jackson. True, Wolfe did capture Quebec City for the British by staging a daring night raid and by climbing sheer cliffs to surprise the French. But he perished several days after the battle of an infection contracted from a wrist wound. That hardly seems a contented way to die.

Bibliography

Adams, Charles. *Roadside Markers in West Virginia*. Shepherdstown, W.Va.: self-published, 1995.

Brown, Canter, Jr. *Fort Meade, 1849-1900*. Tuscaloosa, Ala.: University of Alabama Press, 1995.

Brown, Katharine L. *Stonewall Jackson in Lexington: The Christian Soldier*. Lexington, Va.: Stonewall Jackson Foundation, 1984.

Chambers, Lenoir. *Stonewall Jackson*. 2 vols. New York: William Morrow and Company, 1959.

Cohen, Stan. *Historic Springs of the Virginias: A Pictorial History*. Charleston, W.Va.: Pictorial Histories Publishing Company, 1981.

Current, Richard N., ed. *Encyclopedia of the Confederacy*. 4 vols. New York: Simon and Schuster, 1993.

Davis, Burke. *They Called Him Stonewall: A Life of Lt. General T. J. Jackson, CSA*. New York: Wings Books, 1954.

Early Northampton. Northampton, Mass.: Betty Allen Chapter of the Daughters of the American Revolution, 1914.

Farwell, Byron. *Stonewall: A Biography of Gen. Thomas J. Jackson*. New York: W. W. Norton and Company, 1992.

"Fort Ontario." *Oswego County Department of Promotion and Tourism*. http://www.co.oswego.ny.us/tourism/history-art/fort.html (May 2001).

"General Lee's Visit." *The Miles/LeHane Group, Inc.* 2001. http://www.mileslehane.com/general.html (May 2001).

Happel, Ralph. *The Last Days of Jackson.* Richmond, Va.: Eastern National Park and Memorial Association, 1971.

Heidler, David, and Jeanne Heidler, eds. *Encyclopaedia of the American Civil War.* 5 vols. Santa Barbara, Calif.: ABC-CLIO, 2000.

Hill, Daniel Harvey. *The Real Stonewall Jackson.* http://ourworld.compuserve.com/homepages/Brad_Haugaard/stonewal.htm. (May 2001). This article was first published in *Century Magazine* in February 1894.

Hotchkiss, Jedediah. *Make Me a Map of the Valley: The Civil War Journal of Stonewall Jackson's Topographer.* Dallas, Tex.: Southern Methodist University, 1973.

Jackson, Mary Anna. *Life and Letters of General Thomas J. Jackson.* New York: Harper and Brothers, 1892.

Johnson, Clint. *Touring the Carolinas' Civil War Sites.* Winston-Salem, N.C.: John F. Blair, Publisher, 1996.

————. *Touring Virginia's and West Virginia's Civil War Sites.* Winston-Salem, N.C.: John F. Blair, Publisher, 1999.

Kostyal, K. M. *Stonewall Jackson: A Life Portrait.* Dallas, Tex.: Taylor Publishing Company, 1999.

Mayhurst Inn, The. 1998. http://www.bbonline.com/va/mayhurst/history.html (May 2001).

Norman, Dennis. *Under the Shade of the Trees: Thomas (Stonewall) Jackson's Life at Jackson's Mill.* Charleston, W.Va.: Mountain State Press, 2000.

Porter, Dorothy B. "The Water Cures." In *The Northampton Book*, edited by the Tercentenary History Committee. Northampton, Mass.: Tercentenary History Committee, 1954.

Robertson, James I., Jr. *Stonewall Jackson: The Man, the Soldier, the Legend.* New York: Macmillan, 1997.

Salmon, John, *A Guidebook to Virginia's Historical Markers.* Charlottesville, Va.: University Press of Virginia, 1994.

Shenandoah National Park. http://www.nps.gov/shen/ (May 2001).

Soderberg, Susan Cooke. *A Guide to Civil War Sites in Maryland: Blue and Gray in a Border State.* Shippensburg, Pa.: White Mane Books, 1998.

"Stonewall Jackson Resources." *Virginia Military Institute Archives Home Page*. http://www.vmi.edu/~archtml/ (May 2001).

Tanner, Robert G. *Stonewall in the Valley: Thomas J. "Stonewall" Jackson's Shenandoah Valley Campaign, 1862*. Garden City, N.Y.: Doubleday and Company, 1976.

Waugh, John C. *The Class of 1846, from West Point to Appomattox: Stonewall Jackson, George McClellan and Their Brothers*. New York: Ballantine Books, 1994.

William Wing Loring World Wide Website, The. 1999. http://home.earthlink.net/~atomic_rom/petition.htm (May 2001).

Index

Cold Harbor, Va., 100, 164, 166, 167

Corbin, Jamie, 152-53

Cottage Home, N.C., 191, 194, 195

Cross Keys, Battle of, 93-94

Culpeper, Va., 138, 139

Cumberland, Md., 22

Dabbs House, 159, 160, 162

Dabney, Robert, 135, 158

Dam Number Five, 60, 131, 188, 189, 191

Darksville, W.Va., 29, 32-33

Davidson College, 116, 193

Davis, Jefferson, 25, 61, 79, 81, 162, 170

Delaplane, Va., 72

Dickerson Park, 173

Douglas, Henry Kyd, 43, 178, 180, 181, 188

Dranesville, Va., 36, 87

Dunker Church. *See* German Baptist Brethren

18th North Carolina Regiment, 195-97

Ellwood, 142, 148

Elmwood Cemetery, 41-42

Ewell, Richard, 93, 94, 138, 156, 160

Exchange Hotel Museum, 136, 137

Fairfield, 155

Falling Waters, W.Va., 27-30, 56, 127

Fancy. *See* Little Sorrel

Felix Hull House, 104, 107

Ferry Hill Place, 185

Fort Columbus, N.Y., 212

Fort Hamilton, N.Y., 109, 199, 205, 206

Fort Jay, N.Y. *See* Fort Columbus, N.Y.

Fort Meade, Fla., 186, 198-203

Fort Ontario, N.Y., 209, 220

Fort Putnam, N.Y., 216

Frank Kemper House, 96

Franklin Literary Society, 117, 119-20

Franklin, William, 151

Frayser's Farm, 168

Frederick, Md., 175-81, 182, 188

Fredericks Hall, Va., 135, 158-59, 162, 163

Fredericksburg, Battle of, 69, 143, 149-55

Fremont, John C., 93, 102, 105, 107

French, William, 186, 199, 201, 202, 221

Fritchie, Barbara, 181

Front Royal, Battle of, 90-92, 98

Gaines Mill, Battle of, 166, 167

Gainesboro, W.Va. *See* Pughtown, W.Va.

Garnett, Richard, 23, 67, 138, 139

George Kemper House, 95

German Baptist Brethren, 184, 185, 186

German Reformed Church (Frederick, Md.), 175, 178

Gordonsville Presbyterian Church, 136-37

Gordonsville, Va., 135, 136-37

Governor's Mansion, 160, 162

Grapevine Bridge, 164, 168

Gregg, Maxcy, 151

Griffin, Charles, 77, 78

Grottoes, 136